Going Dark

Guy R. McPherson

PublishAmerica
Baltimore

First printing

PublishAmerica has allowed this work to remain exactly as the author intended, verbatim, without editorial input.

Softcover 9781629074283
PUBLISHED BY PUBLISHAMERICA, LLLP
www.publishamerica.com
Baltimore

Printed in the United States of America

To all those who oppose the well-behaved, small-minded corporate drones who know we have no future and yet still go to their inane desk jobs, attempting to destroy the remaining shards of the living planet

"We can easily forgive a child who is afraid of the dark; the real tragedy of life is when men are afraid of the light."
(Plato)

"Someone I loved once gave me a box full of darkness. It took me years to understand that this too, was a gift."
(Mary Oliver)

"When you light a candle, you also cast a shadow." (Ursula K. Le Guin)

Acknowledgments

Most of the essays in this collection were published as drafts at *Nature Bats Last* (guymcpherson.com). The current collection benefited from the commentary of the erudite readers at that website, as well as from the careful eyes and open minds of Judith Haran, Sheila Merrigan, John Rember, Pauline Schneider, and Mike Sliwa.

TABLE OF CONTENTS

INTRODUCTION.. 11

BIG STUFF 19
ON BEING A RADICAL.. 28
LETTING GO 36
DORMITORY DAYS 44
HOPE IS HOPELESS... 48
THE KNIFE AND THE NUN.. 62
SPREADING THE HORROR... 68
THEATER OF THE ABSURD.. 78
CLIMATE CHAOS IS POISED TO KILL US ALL................... 85
THE ABSURDITY OF AUTHENTICITY................................. 105
IDENTITY CRISIS... 119
THE THIRD INDUSTRIAL REVOLUTION WILL NOT BE
      TELEVISED 132
PLAYING COURT JESTER 138
LET GO, OR BE DRAGGED.. 145
WHAT ARE WE FIGHTING FOR? 151
ONLY LOVE REMAINS 154

INTRODUCTION

My previous ten books have been read by few people, and have therefore had little impact. The grapevine informs me there is a good book in each of us, just waiting to get out. I'm hoping this is mine.

My other books adopted a hopelessly optimistic tone with respect to the most important phenomena in the history of our species. Until recently I believed complete collapse of the world's industrial economy would prevent runaway greenhouse and therefore allow our species to persist a few more generations. But in June 2012 the ocean of evidence on climate change overwhelmed me, and I no longer subscribe to the notion that habitat for humans will exist on Earth beyond the 2030s. We've triggered too many self-reinforcing feedback loops to prevent near-term extinction at our own hand, as I explain in later chapters.

Actually, this was a *deja vu* moment for me. I had reached a similar conclusion in early days of the twenty-first century while editing a book about climate change. About a year after I realized we were "done" and I began mourning the impending loss of our species, I discovered what appeared to be the ultimate hail-Mary pass: the impending peak in global oil production might cause industrial civilization to collapse in time to prevent near-term human extinction. Alas, several years after passing the peak of global oil extraction in 2005 or 2006 (according to the U.S. Energy

Information Administration and International Energy Agency, respectively), the evidence is in: we're done all over again. The mourning began anew for me in June 2012.

Around this same time, I realized that my carefully thought out and constructed living arrangements no longer made any sense. My project of abandoning empire and moving off grid to a shared property in New Mexico has failed catastrophically. Consider the primary reasons I left the easy life of a tenured professor at a major university to develop and occupy the property I call the mud hut:

(1) an act of resistance against the dominant paradigm (the dominant paradigm and those within it failed to notice);

(2) an example of alternative living, in my case promoting a gift economy within agrarian anarchy (my example has failed to inspire a significant number of others to live differently);

(3) a way to provide more time for speaking and writing about important topics, actions that were discouraged at the university (I have enjoyed limited success in this arena, although time freed up not battling administrative dragons has been largely consumed with rigorous physical work);

(4) a refuge for the youngster, the son of the couple with whom my wife and I share this property, as well as his generation (due to ongoing, accelerating climate change, the youngster's future in this location probably will be notably short), and

(5) a way to extend my own life, and that of my wife (due to ongoing, accelerating climate change, our future in this location is likely to be quite short).

Perhaps most importantly, there is a widening chasm within the partnership formed on this shared property. Although leaving the life I loved as an academic to move to this location made sense at the time, long before the climate-change news grew so dire and when collapse appeared imminent, I now view the major personal transition as infinitely regrettable. I have come to see it as the worst mistake of my life, so far. I'm not dead, though, so I suspect I can yet outdo myself.

Looking back on my enormous effort and life-changing transition, it seems that perhaps our choice of homesteading partners was doomed to fail. Partnerships of all sorts fail more often than not (consider, for example, the divorce rate in the United States). The choice of partners for constructing a viable off-grid homestead is perhaps even more crucial than the choice of one's spouse.

My attempt to walk away from empire has failed in part because empire is stunningly difficult to leave behind. The disaster of American imperialism follows like the "evil twin" of a beloved dog: You know something is dogging your heels, but it's no longer your loving companion. I'm left with the horrors of American Empire and the abyss of near-term human extinction without my long-time canine friend.

The sun sets

One day short of a full year after I re-reached the conclusion about near-term human extinction, darkness fell again. My canine companion of nearly 16 years, Savanna Louise Rose O'Malley McPherson, died on 19 June 2013 while my wife and I were in an airplane en route to a family wedding. Her most recent photo, taken just hours before leaving on our trip, smiled back at me on my computer. Overwhelmed, I dove deeply into despair yet again.

Way back when, my family had a dog as I was growing up. Shorty arrived when I was in elementary school. A short, homely terrier of dubious heritage, she was an excellent, adventurous traveler. She loved camping and was truly an integral part of the family until she died during my college years.

My wife and I held out for a long time before we felt sufficiently mature and financially stable to have a pet of our own. Shortly after we moved into our first non-rental home—and so far, only one of two we've owned—we adopted a recently weaned puppy from the Humane Society in Tucson. Ever the rationalist, I insisted upon several criteria before we viewed the available dogs: female, puppy, short hair, light color, about 50 pounds fully grown.

When my wife walked into the room with available dogs, she settled on the first animal that entered her view. I consider myself lucky she didn't first see a hippopotamus, although we did adopt a black, Doberman-German Shepherd mix that achieved nearly 100 pounds in weight.

Mancha (Spanish for "Spot") quickly became our constant companion. She walked us twice daily in the Sonoran Desert near our small, suburban home. She took us hiking and camping and, like my childhood dog, became very much a part of me.

Mancha was diagnosed with bone cancer at about a year of age, and she died shortly after her second birthday. We approved chemotherapy and radiation therapy, and we held on too long. When Mancha died, she nearly took me with her: If I'd have had a handgun at my disposal, I would've used it on myself. The grief was horrible, and thinking about Mancha still brings tears to my eyes today, more than twenty years after her death.

My wife was devastated too, and we waited a long time before considering another pet. I dragged her to the Humane Society a mere seven years after our initial visit.

This time, my wife stayed in the car. A friend went inside with me, and the criteria remained largely the same. We were willing to take an adult, but we desired a female, short-haired, light-colored companion that weighed about 50 pounds fully grown. After checking every dog at the Humane Society, we ventured to the county animal facility (the "pound"). And then we went back to the Humane Society. Fortunately, the dog I spied on the first trip was still there an hour later.

My friend and I took the female, short-haired, brindle-and-white dog outside to meet my wife, knowing she would approve. Seeing four legs and fur, she did. We were informed the unnamed dog was between six months and two years of age, so we arbitrarily decided that day, 21 June 1997, was adoption day and her first birthday.

Savanna Louise Rose O'Malley McPherson
Whereas Mancha was named with local heritage in mind, Savanna received her name from my primary study system. I was a field ecologist working primarily on southwestern oak savannas, and Savanna spent her early years as my constant field companion. She took us on twice-daily walks in our Sonoran Desert home, and ventured into the field with me constantly. She was an ideal adventurer, accompanying us to the Washington, D.C. metropolitan area for a leave of absence as I helped establish the world's premiere postdoctoral program (The

Smith Fellows program is currently administered by the Society for Conservation Biology), and then to the campus of Grinnell College (Iowa) for a short teaching stint, and finally to The Nature Conservancy property where I took my final sabbatical leave from the University of Arizona.

Savanna was a natural-born hunter. She accumulated at least 14 vertebrate species on her life kill list, including a skunk (pure persistence), two species of cottontail rabbit (pure speed), three species of lizard (pure quickness), and a quail—in flight, on a nature preserve (pure embarrassment, for me).

Savanna was a warrior, and she was also a witness. She saw my transition from earnest ecologist to cynical social critic. She saw my transformation from hard-working, little-rewarded, 37-year-old associate professor to thoughtful, well-respected, 53-year-old professor. She was present for the end of the age of economic expansion and the beginning of the age of contraction. She traveled thousands of miles and enriched the lives of hundreds of humans and other animals (although admittedly not those many individuals whose lives she terminated).

At the age of ten years, Savanna's knees went south. She'd already had minor surgery on one wrist. And, thanks to a collision with a cactus spine while chasing prey, she came within less than one-hundredth of an inch of losing the vitreous humor from one eye, according to the astonished eye specialist. But knee surgery is serious business. We opted for tibial plateau leveling osteotomy (TPLO), an incredibly invasive and disruptive process with an excellent record of full recovery. Savanna's recovery was rapidly complete seven full years ago.

On Thanksgiving Day 2012, Savanna suffered numerous puncture wounds under her chin, though we did not see them that day. The following morning, 23 November 2012, her head and neck suddenly swelled. A lot. The emergency veterinarian barely glanced at her, concluded a venomous snake was the likely culprit, and sent us along our way. The serious bleeding from the puncture wounds beneath Savanna's chin began three days later, by which time Savanna had been transported to a reliable veterinarian in Tucson. I knew these were her final days.

I was mistaken, fortunately, reminding me of one of my undesirable traits: frequently in error, but never in doubt. The puncture wounds did not result from a snake, though the source was never identified. Against all odds, Savanna recovered and carried on for another seven months. As my wife and I were caught between flights in an airport, we received the news: The friend who helped me select Savanna sixteen years ago came home to check on the dog we left in her care. The Best Dog Ever died in her sleep 19 June 2013, two days short of her seventeenth birthday.

When we received the news in the airport, we tried to arrange an immediate trip back home. Alas, we were too late for the last flight back to Tucson. We spent time with the living and returned home to the body of our best friend a few days later.

All in all, Savanna experienced the Gonzo life described by Hunter S. Thompson: "Life should not be a journey to the grave with the intention of arriving safely in a pretty and well preserved body, but rather to skid in broadside in a cloud of smoke, thoroughly used up, totally worn out, and loudly proclaiming 'Wow! What a Ride!'" We should all be so lucky. Although our lives have been forever enriched by

Savanna Louise Rose O'Malley McPherson, good luck isn't on my mind as I think of her.

As suggested by the title of this book, this text is not for the faint of heart. Not only are the lights about to go out on industrial civilization, but the lights are about to go out on our species. Marching in lockstep with the dark days faced by society and *Homo sapiens* is my own heart, heavy with the knowledge in my head and the failure of my personal efforts. My prose in this work reflects the darkness of our final days. It's time to learn to let go, one last time.

BIG STUFF

When man interferes with the Tao,
the sky becomes filthy,
the earth becomes depleted,
the equilibrium crumbles
creatures become extinct
(Lao Tzu, *Tao Te Ching*, ca. 550 BCE)

Shortly after the arrival of the 21st century I realized we were putting the finishing touches on our own extinction party, with the shindig probably over within a few decades. During the intervening period I've seen nothing to sway this belief, and much evidence to reinforce it. Yet the protests, ridicule, and hate mail reach a fervent pitch when I speak or write about the potential for near-term extinction of *Homo sapiens*. I hear how:

We're different.

We're special.

We're too intelligent.

We'll find a way out. We always do.

We're humans, and therefore animals. Like all life, we're special. Like all organisms, we're susceptible to overshoot. Like all organisms, we will experience population decline after overshoot. Given our tremendous ability to abuse our tremendous power, we will not only drive other species to extinction, but instead will take ourselves into the darkest of existential nights.

For my initial forty years on Earth, I was an unrepentant idealist. Surrounded by students I loved, pursuing a life of excellence rooted in inquiry, striving to serve humanity and the living planet, I cared about humans and other species to the point of heartbreak. I pinned my dreams on people and believed they would rise to the occasion. No more. Color me cynical in the spirit of comedian George Carlin, who died in 2008: "Scratch any cynic and you will find a disappointed idealist."

I also spent my first forty years saving for a rainy day. My wife and I lived on one-third of our combined income and socked away plenty of fiat currency for the retirement of leisure we had in our dreams. Looking back through the lenses of knowledge and cynicism, it all seems so surreal.

Let's take stock of our current predicaments, beginning with one of several ongoing processes likely to cause our extinction. Then I'll point out the good news. Or, rather, the not-quite-so-bad news.

We're headed for extinction via global climate change
It's hotter than it used to be, but not as hot as it's going to be. The political response to this now-obvious information is to ignore or disparage the scientist bearing the bad news. Which, of course, is no surprise at all: Not only would any politician who openly contemplates economic contraction shortly find herself out of a job, but discussing human extinction likely would elicit laughter and calls for tar and feathers.

Climate change is one of three likely extinction events. Well, three I know about: I'm certain there are others, and any number can play. Because climate change represents a profound and growing threat to *Homo sapiens*, an entire chapter is dedicated to its elucidation (**Climate Chaos is Poised to Kill Us All**).

We're headed for extinction via environmental collapse
The human role in extinction of species and degradation of ecosystems is well documented. Since European settlement in North America, and especially after the beginning of the Industrial Revolution, we have witnessed a substantial decline in biological diversity of native taxa and profound changes in assemblages of the remaining species. We have ripped minerals from the Earth, often bringing down mountains in the process; we have harvested nearly all the old-growth timber on the continent, replacing thousand-year-old trees with neatly ordered plantations of small trees; we have hunted species to the point of extinction; we have driven livestock across almost every acre of the continent, baring hillsides and facilitating massive erosion; we have plowed large landscapes, transforming fertile soil into sterile, lifeless dirt; we have burned ecosystems and, perhaps more importantly, we have extinguished naturally occurring fires; we have paved thousands of acres to facilitate our movement and, in the process, have disrupted the movements of thousands of species; we have spewed pollution and dumped garbage, thereby dirtying our air, fouling our water, and contributing greatly to the warming of the planet. We have, to the maximum possible extent allowed by our intellect and never-ending desire, consumed the planet. In the wake of these endless insults to our only home, perhaps the greatest surprise is that so many

native species have persisted, thus allowing our continued enjoyment and exploitation.

Every other nation on Earth doggedly pursues America. As a result, nature has joined Wall Street and every country in the industrialized world in bankruptcy. Thanks for playing, but you lose. The banksters on Wall Street "win," but only in the very short term. In the long run, we're all dead (as first stated by British economist John Maynard Keynes). And, in the current case, the long run is rather short.

Among the consequences of taking down a few hundred species each day: at some point, we are the species we take into the abyss. The vanishing point draws nearer every day. Our response, in the industrialized world: Bring on the toys. Burn all fossil fuels. Harvest the rain forests and strip-mine the soil. Pollute the water, eat the seed bank. Foul the air.

And, most importantly, figure out how we can make a few bucks as the world burns.

We have our hand in a monkey trap, and we can't let go. A monkey trap is a small cage with a piece of fruit inside, anchored to a solid object. The cage has a hole barely large enough for a monkey to insert its empty hand, but too small to extract the hand holding a piece of fruit. The monkey is trapped, unable to let go of the fruit. In our case, the trap holds the low-hanging fruit of empire: cheap water, cheap food, cheap fossil fuels, and cheap toys. *Homo sapiens*—literally, the "wise" ape—is enamored with all things cheap, up to and including life itself.

We're headed for extinction via nuclear meltdown
Safely shuttering a nuclear power plant requires a decade or two of careful planning. Far sooner, we'll complete the

ongoing collapse of the industrial economy. This is a source of my nuclear nightmares.

When the world's 440 or so nuclear power plants melt down catastrophically, we've entered an extinction event. Think clusterfukushima, raised to the power of a hundred or so. Ionizing radiation could, and probably will, destroy most terrestrial organisms and, therefore, most marine and freshwater organisms. That, by the way, includes the most unique, special, intelligent animal on Earth.

"Good" news

Oil discovery and extraction tend to follow bell-shaped curves, as described by petroleum geologist M. King Hubbert in a presentation he delivered in 1956. The easily reached, light oil is extracted first. Heavier oil, often characterized by high sulfur content, is found at greater depths on land and also offshore. This heavier oil requires more money and more energy to extract and to refine than light oil. Eventually, all fields and regions become unviable economically and energetically. When extracting a barrel of oil requires more energy than contained in the barrel of oil, extraction is pointless.

The top of the bell-shaped curve for oil extraction is called "Peak Oil" or "Hubbert's Peak." We passed Hubbert's Peak for world oil supply in 2005 or 2006 (according to the U.S. Department of Energy's Energy Information Administration and the International Energy Agency, respectively). In response, conventional crude oil has been replaced with liquid substitutes such as tar sands and hydro-fractured shale, the costs of which go well beyond financial.

The ongoing recession of the world's industrial economy results from the high price of oil and has led to a reduction in demand for oil and numerous other finite commodities, hence leading to reduced prices since the price of crude peaked at $147.27 per barrel in July 2008. Many geologists and scientists predict a permanent economic depression will result from declining availability of oil and the associated dramatic swings in the price of oil. It seems clear we're locked into a permanent economic emergency. The absence of a politically viable solution to energy decline explains, at least in part, the absence of a governmental response to the issue even though governments of the world recognize peak oil as a serious problem.

Without energy, societies collapse. In contemporary, industrialized societies, virtually all energy sources are derived from oil. Even "renewable" energy sources such as hydropower, wind turbines, and solar panels require an enormous amount of oil for construction, maintenance, and repair. Extraction and delivery of coal, natural gas, and uranium similarly are oil-intensive endeavors. Thus, the decline of inexpensive oil spells economic disaster for industrialized countries. Demand destruction caused by high energy prices is affecting the entire industrialized world.

Viewed from a broader perspective than energy, economic collapses result from an imbalance between demand and supply of one or more resources (as explained in considerable depth by Jared Diamond in his 2005 book, *Collapse: How Societies Choose to Fail or Succeed*). When supply of vital materials is outstripped by demand, governments often print currency, which leads to hyperinflation. In recent history, the price of oil and its refined products have been primary to rates of inflation and have played central roles in the maintenance of civilized societies.

Addressing the issue of peak oil while also controlling emissions of carbon dioxide, and therefore reducing the prospect of "runaway greenhouse" on planet Earth, represented a challenge we failed to overcome. Peak oil and the attendant collapse of industrial civilization failed to mitigate in time the effects of runaway greenhouse, nuclear Armageddon, and environmental decay. In the short run, having passed the world oil peak leads to imminent disaster for civilization and those who depend upon it. In the slightly longer run, the other crises on the list lead to human extinction.

If you're looking for a personal response to the converging crises in which we're immersed, you could do worse than recognizing reality. And then, let go. Revel in the uniqueness that is the human experience. Acknowledge the wonder of your life, part of which—admittedly, the last part—is your death.

Again I invoke the wisdom of George Carlin: "When you're born into this world, you're given a ticket to the freak show. If you're born in America you get a front row seat."

And then what?

As ecologist Garrett Hardin pointed out long before his death more than a decade ago, the ecologically literate question is, "And then what?" Anybody interested in individual or societal action must be willing to answer this question. With respect to ongoing depletion of fossil fuels, any response to Hardin's question must include the matter of scale. Individuals are able to abandon fossil fuels before they abandon us. Doing so with grace is a bit challenging, but it's hardly impossible. Contemporary industrialized societies, on the other hand, are exhibiting little interest in adapting to a world without ready access to inexpensive fossil fuels. Apparently the people pulling the primary levers of industry would rather continue fighting than switch to a saner way of living.

Individuals are able to abandon a fossil-fuel-fueled lifestyle with minor costs, including the disparagement that comes from living outside the mainstream. But, as illustrated by Jevons' paradox and the Khazzoom-Brookes postulate, individual choices do not translate to societal choices. An individual change in consciousness rarely leads to societal enlightenment. Jumping off the cruise ship of empire will not prevent the ship from striking the iceberg, and it nonetheless results in near-term death of the individual.

If we're headed for the exit gate in the near term, the question then arises: What shall I do? How shall I live my life? In other words, now that we have knowledge of the near-term demise of our species, then what? There are more than seven billion responses to the latter questions. Recognizing that birth is lethal and that we have an opportunity to demonstrate our humanity on the way out the door, I've chosen an eyes-wide-open, decidedly counter-cultural approach. I've opted out of empire to the maximum possible extent, and I practice and promote a gift economy. Beyond my own actions, I suggest individuals take actions they never previously imagined. I promote resistance against the dominant paradigm, even though—especially though—it appears too late to save our species from near-term extinction. I propose assaulting ourselves and others with compassion. I recommend heavy doses of creativity and courage. I advise doing something well beyond the cultural current of the main stream. At this point, what have you got to lose? Indeed, what have *we* got to lose?

ON BEING A RADICAL

You probably recognize this symbol, though you might have forgotten its name: √

When I write the symbol on the whiteboard in a class, and ask what it is, the response is invariable: "The square root."

I respond, "Yes, its function is to take the root, including the square root or any other root. But what is it called?"

Extended silence ensues, followed by, "The square-root symbol."

I lead the abundant laughter.

"Really? Nobody took math in junior high?"

Nervous laughter.

"I've insulted everybody here within the first minute of our meeting," I say. "Now that that's out of the way, let's proceed."

I allow a long pause before I give away the answer: "It's called a radical." Another long pause before I reveal the point of this exercise. "It's called a radical because it gets at the root. That, by the way, is the definition of radical: of or going to the root or origin."

I use this anecdote to introduce myself to the class. I'm a radical, I point out. And, whereas this culture has convinced most people that a radical is a bad thing, similarly to anarchy, it's actually a very good thing, and it's different than most people believe.

On this topic, the words of H. L. Mencken resonate with me: "The notion that a radical is one who hates his country is naive and usually idiotic. He is, more likely, one who likes his country more than the rest of us, and is thus more disturbed than the rest of us when he sees it debauched. He is not a bad citizen turning to crime; he is a good citizen driven to despair."

A good citizen driven to despair. That sounds about right. A few excerpts demonstrate the point:

The perfect parrot was the perfect pupil...As students in grammar school or in high school we seldom question the truth of any statement. Instead, our concern was to get each phrase exactly as the teacher or textbook stated it...Imagine the effect of years of such training on the developing mind. The habit of mental conformity becomes almost ineradicable. I was merely one of generations of victims. How many teachers suggested to us that the established order was not all that it might be? Even the possibility of change was hinted at only vaguely. We were not rebels. We were not pioneers. We were not even enthusiastic or devout copyists. We were mere discs on which the language of our generation was cut. At certain intervals, called examination periods, we were expected to reproduce this language, word by word and paragraph by paragraph.

The American Way was not based on "life, liberty and the pursuit of happiness," but upon the determination of business men to hold down wages and push up profits. The American Way was designed to make the rich richer while it kept the poor in their places.

Meanwhile the war makers, whose profession is wholesale destruction and mass murder, had taken over control of the United States and its policies, were writing the words, calling the tune...The United States of my youth was slipping from under my feet and vanishing from my sight. The Mayflower Covenant, William Penn's charter of love and good human relations, Thomas Jefferson's Bill of Rights, the Constitution of 1789 which as a schoolboy I had learned word for word, Lincoln's Gettysburg Address and Second Inaugural had become obsolete scraps of paper...We had begun beating our plowshares into swords and our pruning hooks into spears, transforming tools into weapons and techniques of destruction and murder.

Where did I belong? How could I classify myself? Was I a Don Quixote, tilting ineffectually at windmills? Was I crazy and were my stand-pat conservative fellow citizens sane? Was I alone sane and they all off the track?

This world I saw was not at all to my liking. It was a world in which the destructive forces clearly had the upper hand. I had been taught to believe in the possibilities of well-being for every individual and the probability of social improvement. I found myself in a world hell-bent on its own destruction.

I live in the United States only because my post of duty is there...I am ashamed of any connection with the oligarchy which presently misgoverns, exploits, plunders, and corrupts the United States and the world.

As an individual, I continue to do what I can. I go about, talk, and write in the face of ignorance, inertia, escapism. I believe there is a growing awareness of the crisis and the gravity of the menace hanging over humanity. There is also a growing awareness that the crucial decision has been made and that the process of vaporizing western civilization is well under way...My personal contribution is increasingly a form of foreign aid—a contribution to fellow citizens whom I seem not to know. They are a people without history, misled, deluded, inexperienced, baffled. They are people who are turning more and more away from reason and foresight to instinct, emotion, and pathetically desperate efforts to escape a fate that is closing in around them as a fog envelops a ship at sea.

With increasing awareness of the real situation there has grown up in me a conviction that I should do something about it. I have tried talking, writing, speaking, lecturing, and have been bypassed and ignored by my fellow Americans. I continue to do what I can, at every opportunity. I have spoken my lines as I have thought them out and learned them. I continue to offer my help to my fellow Americans as one would offer help to a drowning man who every moment is being carried farther away by an irresistible current. I offer this aid gladly, hopefully, anxiously.

Like the Ancient Mariner, I am saying to preoccupied passersby: you have chosen and are following a path that leads to your destruction and probably to the destruction of hundreds of millions of your fellows. I have advised, opposed, warned, decried, denounced. You continue on your way to perdition. You rush on, unheeding. I continue to warn. You do not look and do not listen. You do not see the infinitely rich possibilities of life, lying unused at your feet. You go your own way—the way that millions of humans have gone before you, lured and corrupted by the glass beads and printed calicos which civilized societies offers to its devotees.

I have turned my back on the American Oligarchy, the American Way of Life, and American Century, the American Empire, western civilization. The entire chain of civilizations have brought a little light, learning, joy, and hope to a very few human beings while multitudes lived and died in darkness, ignorance, misery, despair. I have turned my back on this short-sighted, opportunistic acceptance of that which is, because I am convinced that we could reach out, create, touch, and grasp a better life and make it ours, if only we would put forth the effort.

I have burned the last bridge which connected me with the American Way of Life because I am convinced that the ideas, devices, techniques, and institutions of civilization have been tried time after time and found wanting. They are superfluous and obsolete because better ways are already in being, available to any who will turn their backs on the past and face the future hopefully, confidently, creatively, and conscious of the need for concerted, radical action.

I say farewell to western civilization. With no shadow of regret I try to dismiss it from my life as I try to dismiss any other unsavory, painful memory.

My separation from western civilization and its ways is almost as complete as my separation from the civilizations of Rome and Egypt. I continue to live in the United States, the power center of western civilization because this is part of my assignment, but I have no more sympathy with it or concern for it than an emissary of the United States has in a precapitalist area—no plural of equatorial Africa or South America. The emissary lives in the midst of backwardness, but is not of it. This is exactly my feeling about my relations with the United States, in which perforce I must live.

Who could have imagined in the early part of the century that after a brief foreign sojourn I would return to these shores and find large sections of Los Angeles, Detroit, and Washington smoking ruins, sacked, and looted? Who could have foreseen the mounting drug addiction among the population, the vicious crime waves, the riots, the police ferocity? Each time I asked myself, incredulously, can this be home?

The affluent, drugged, debauched, corrupted, polluted, deluded nation is a country I never envisioned in my youth. It is an alien and hostile land. When I return to it I cannot say happily, "I am going home." Instead, I must gird myself and prepare to return to a foreign and none too pleasant habitat.

No thoughtful person can face the facts of present-day life without realizing the terrible urgency of the situation. It is the dawning of this realization that is largely responsible for the tidal wave of protest, disruption, and destruction that is presently sweeping over the planet. The reaction is more evident among young people. They have their lives ahead of them. The parents, members of the previous generation, are more inured to the situation. Most of them never had it so good.

Man disturbs and upsets the balance of nature. Nature retorts by restoring the balance. From childhood to man's estate we construct dams and dykes. Before we turn our backs nature is undermining and breaching. Water is again running downhill. Nature is tireless, persistent, implacable.

Teaching is my job. Teaching, in its largest sense means searching out the truth, telling it to all who are willing to learn, and building it into the life of the community. Truth is often unpleasant, annoying, and unpalatable to those who hold a disproportionate amount of worldly goods, who are power hungry, and who are pushing a cause to the detriment of the many. So they try to avoid truth, to cover it up, to forget it. It is the job of the teaching profession, of which I have been a lifetime member, to keep on uncovering the truth, reminding the rich and powerful of its character and its significance, bringing it to public attention, and arguing that it be made the cornerstone of local, regional, national and planet-wide public life.

I have had the rare privilege of being present, and of assisting slightly, at the death process of one social system and through the early stages of the development of an alternative pattern of human society. If this were all that life had granted me it would be a lifetime well spent. I am grateful for the opportunity and hopeful that my fellowmen will carry on to victory in the perilous fight, taking fuller and fuller advantage of the infinite possibilities for creative experiment and persistent improvement.

The preceding words, like those of Mencken, resonate with me. They were written by Scott Nearing and published in 1972 in his autobiography, *The Making of a Radical*. He was 89 years old at the time. References to his youth and to the early part of the century offer his perspective from the early 1900s.

A full century later, I am afflicted with a form of radicalism similar to that which plagued Nearing. I am ignored or disparaged when I point out the actions taken to prop up an empire in decline, including requisite obedience at home, horrific oppression abroad, and wholesale destruction of the living planet.

Too, I am ignored or disparaged when I point out the obvious signs of human-population overshoot and the likely near-term results, as well as the root causes of overshoot. To be fair, I'm hardly alone when I criticize civilization as a sickness. The catcalls increase in number and tenacity when I point out the seemingly obvious need to destroy industrial civilization, the system that is driving to extinction several hundred species each day while making us sick, driving us to insanity, and killing us while we further human-population overshoot and the despoiling of our only home.

Imagine this scenario: You walk past a house every day. In the house, an old man kills 200 human babies as you stroll by. What shall you do? The response to which I've become accustomed: You walk past the house, plugging your ears to the screams and closing your eyes to the sights.

It's not a hypothetical scenario, and it's far worse than I've indicated. It's not merely 200 human babies this old civilization is killing every day. It's 200 *species*. In other words, it's genocide. The majority responds by wishing this omnicidal system will continue forever. A slim minority wish it will end, thereby leaving habitat for humans for another few years. Vanishingly few people are motivated to the type of action that might preserve life, including habitat for humans.

How radical are you? Do you love life? Are you willing to fight for it? Are you willing to take action to save non-human species?

LETTING GO

I had the brass ring. And I let it go. I had reached the pinnacle of the educational world: I was a tenured full professor by the age of 40. I walked away from that life, which I loved, an act that made most people think I'd lost my mind. I'll not rule that out, but I want to tell you my side of the story anyway.

After trying to change the morally bankrupt system in which we are all immersed, I realized the system was changing me, and not for the better. So I let go when I realized the first step I could take toward destroying this irredeemably corrupt system was to leave it. I hope you come to understand some of the disadvantages of industrial civilization. If you do, I invite you to join me in letting go of the many advantages of living within an empire.

The beginning of the story is an important part, so I'll start much earlier than you'll appreciate—with my birth, in fact, though I won't get into the bloody details.

Born into captivity

Born into captivity and assimilated into the normalcy bias of a historically abnormal period in world history, I did all the things this culture expected from me. For example, I began my career in the expected manner: I was a classroom conservative. I even taught my dog to whistle (she was a terrible student). I received accolades and numerous awards for teaching, advising, and scholarship. Early on, I realized students don't care what you know until they know you care—about them. And I did, in ways that made my colleagues question whose side I was on even while I was pointing out that, in educating ourselves and others, we're all on the same side. Those of us born into an imperial set of living arrangements are hard-pressed to see the advantages of cooperation, or even to recognize that our many similarities bring us together.

Even though I taught, and taught, and taught, my dog never did learn to whistle, which showed me something important: Even earnest, caring teaching doesn't necessarily lead to learning. The Sage on the Stage approach is dead. So, too, is the model of student as customer. So I switched my approach to one based on a "Corps of Discovery" in which every participant is expected to contribute to the learning of every other participant. We practiced anarchism, in our own classroom-centered way, taking responsibility for ourselves and our neighbors. This radical approach to teaching puts it all on the line: Everything I know, and everything I am, is exposed during every meeting of every class. How can we evaluate our knowledge, our wisdom, and own personal growth without exposing our assumptions at every turn? This, of course, requires us to let go: to let go of our hubris, and replace it with humility. To let go of our egos, and instead seek compassion and perhaps even empathy.

We're all on the same side. We are the ones we've been waiting for, as the saying goes, but we must let go of a system that is making us sick, making us crazy, and killing us. During my entire life, and doubtless long before, success has been defined, incorrectly, by the amount of money a person has, rather than the amount of compassion.

Similarly, the entire system has been defined in terms that make no sense because the system rewards money over happiness, and death over life. As John Ralston Saul pointed out in his 1992 book *Voltaire's Bastards*, "never has failure been so ardently defended as success."

Alas, there's good news, too

Fortunately, we're headed to a world where money doesn't matter. And without money, we'll all be rich in the life-sustaining ways that really matter. We spent the first couple million years of the human experience immersed in gift economy, and it seems we'll be there again in the not-too-distant future. I long for the day we see more free-flowing rivers every year, as well as more clean air, more wild places, fewer species driven to extinction, and less soil washed into the world's oceans, each and every year. Regardless how short this period persists in concert with human beings to serve as witnesses, the good news is on its way.

Like me, everybody in the industrialized world was born into captivity. A few people seem to be acknowledging the bars imprisoning them. The unseen bars of our prisons are keeping us from becoming fully human, from fully expressing our humanity. As Goethe said some two centuries ago, "None are more hopelessly enslaved than those who falsely believe they are free." It's time for a jailbreak. Better yet, it's time to heed the words of Joan Baez and raze, raze the prisons to the ground. Even and especially the invisible prisons.

Getting personal

In the latter years of my 20-year stint at the University of Arizona, I was doing the best and most important work of my life. Excluded from teaching in my home department, I taught through a program housed at the university called *Poetry Inside/Out.* "Inside" included the men's pods of the county jail and the girl's pods of the county juvenile detention facility; "Out" included an alternative, vocational high school and my college honors course.

We asked each honors student to pay a visit to the juvenile detention facility. You would be hard-pressed to come up with similar-aged people in this country who had more disparate backgrounds than upper-middle-class, white honors students on the one hand and poor, Latina detainees on the other. The typical detainee is a 15-year-old Hispanic substance abuser who has been subjected to every conceivable kind of abuse, most recently sexual abuse by her mother's current boyfriend. She's been knifed and shot at and she's had a friend die in her arms. Nearly all these events, of course, stemmed from factors largely beyond her control.

After an honors student's first visit to detention, we would ask a single question: "What do you think?" After a minute of reflection, the answer was nearly unanimous among the dozens of honors students: "They're just like me."

Finally, my teaching was inclusive and it led to real learning: empathy is the most important thing we can learn. I'd like to think we were—collectively and individually—living this line from Eugene V. Debs, five-time Socialist Party candidate for president of the U.S.: "While there is a lower class I am in it, while there is a criminal element I am of it; while there is a soul in prison, I am not free." Debs knew that rights are not given, they are fought for; like Thomas Jefferson, Debs knew our rights had to be earned with frequent battles, or they would slip away. Like Jefferson, Debs knew some people must be willing to die to secure other peoples' rights.

Well before this point, my scholarship had broadened to include the twin sides of the fossil-fuel coin—global climate change and peak oil—and my message increasingly targeted the public that was paying my salary. Long a conservation biologist, I had become a friend of the Earth as well as a social critic. And I'd come to recognize the costs and consequences of the industrial economy: obedience at home, oppression abroad, and wholesale destruction of the living planet on which we depend for our very lives.

How do we respond?

As Arundhati Roy wrote in her 2001 book, *Power Politics*: "The trouble is that once you see it, you can't unsee it. And once you've seen it, keeping quiet, saying nothing, becomes as political an act as speaking out. There's no innocence. Either way, you're accountable."

I saw it, and I recognized my accountability. Even though I was doing exceptional work, and doing it well, I was participating in an immoral system. For me, it was time to let go because I could no longer both participate in the system and look at the face in the mirror. I could no longer expose the dark underbelly of civilization and live at the apex of empire. By this time, I had come to recognize that my generation's legacy—the curse my generation leaves behind—is a world depleted of resources, ruined by Empire, and ruled by fascism masquerading as democracy.

In my earlier writings, I put my own spin on Arundhati Roy's conclusion: "Big Energy poisons our water. Big Ag controls our seeds, hence our food. Big Pharma controls, through pharmaceuticals, the behavior of our children. Wall Street controls the flow of money. Big Ad controls the messages we receive every day. The criminally rich get richer through crime: that's how America works. Through it all, we believe we're free."

Like most contemporary Americans, I believed I was free far too long. But in fact I was bound by the monkey trap. A monkey trap is a small cage with a piece of fruit inside, anchored to a solid object. The cage has a hole barely large enough for a monkey to insert its empty hand, but too small to extract the hand holding a piece of fruit. The monkey is trapped, unable to let go of the fruit.

I had the low-hanging fruit of American Empire. Finally, I let go.

Finally, letting go

I miss many aspects of my former life, notably including frequent interaction with inmates and honors students. I miss fingers that open and close on command—my fingers worked fine when all they had to do was corral electrons on a computer monitor—real work, though, induces real, lasting pain. I miss the easy life of civilization, even knowing what it does to the living planet.

The aching in my heart is profound, but it pales in comparison to the heartache I feel when I think about civilization. Industrial civilization forces us to extend human-population overshoot on an overcrowded planet, to the tune of more than 200,000 more people each day. Industrial civilization forces us to overheat our only, already overheated home, setting records every year for greenhouse-gas emissions long after we've understood the consequences. Industrial civilization forces us to ratchet up the Sixth Great Extinction as we drive some 200 species to extinction each and every life-destroying day. And now, with full knowledge that extinction is forever, we are driving our own species to extinction. No matter how badly I miss my former life, I could never go back. And not just because I'd never be hired into a civilized job. But also because modern civilization has just become too insane for me to take.

As I pound away at this keyboard in September 2013, my wife and I share a small property with another small family of humans, as well as goats, ducks, chickens, and gardens. Living in agrarian anarchy, I've taken responsibility for myself and my neighbors, human and otherwise.

Like a Cheyenne dog soldier, I've placed my picket-pin in a small valley at the edge of empire. I will protect this valley, even with my life, from further insults of industry, including the dam proposed near my new home. The problem with being a martyr: you have to die for the cause.

Finally, very late in an unexamined life, I came to see the horrors of the way we live, and I let go. I invite you to join me. And I'd like to raise the stakes by pointing out, yet again, the dire straits in which we find ourselves and the attendant necessity to take action. Taking action will almost certainly bring personal hardship. Acting against the industrial economy brands you a terrorist. It might lead to incarceration and torture, and perhaps even early death. A phrase from activist-writer Derrick Jensen comes to mind: We have the best excuse in the world to not act. So we can have the best excuse in the world, or we can have a world.

With that trade-off in mind, we need witnesses and we need warriors on behalf of the living planet. So, I'd like to extend another invitation. Don't just join me in walking away. Join me as a witness and a warrior, on behalf of life. Ultimately, in other words, on behalf the organisms we leave in our wake as we exit the planetary stage. Because we're on track to cause our own extinction in the near future, and even though the omnicidal culture we know as industrial civilization is about to reach its overdue end, it's long past time to let go of a system that enslaves us all while destroying all life and therefore all that matters. And it's not merely time to let go, but to terminate this increasingly violent system that values the property of the rich more than the lives of the poor.

DORMITORY DAYS

Like many people, I served time in a college dormitory.

Although I grew up in a backwoods, redneck logging town in northern Idaho, my educationally inclined parents steered me away from dangerous jobs working in the woods and, ultimately, toward the academic life. Ergo the opportunity to spend a summer beyond sight of my racist, misogynist contemporaries at the age of 17.

Hot to hotter

From a region filled with white people, characterized by male white privilege, and dominated by fear of "others," I flew to Greenville, North Carolina. There, I spent the summer of 1977 on the campus of East Carolina University surrounded by people who looked different from me. I shared a dorm room with an African American student as tall and skinny as I was. He hailed from Washington, D.C.

We studied physics, pursued the young women in the program, pulled ridiculous pranks on our peers, and played basketball all summer. Despite our obvious differences, we had a lot to talk about. After we parted ways, I never heard from or about Michael again. But, without trying, he changed my life for the better.

From campus we proceeded into downtown Greenville via the sidewalk along a primary street one sultry afternoon. Maria from the Philippines accompanied me, while clinging to Michael's arm was Emily, a blonde, blue-eyed, Caucasian woman. We weren't a block from campus when racial epithets came from a passing muscle car.

Out of the frying pan and into the fire. Hate wasn't restricted to northern Idaho. Three of us were horrified. Michael, familiar with the experience, acted as if it hadn't happened.

Awareness isn't nirvana. It's hell.

College bound

Driving as far as I could from my hometown while still availing myself of a generous scholarship from the state of Idaho, I pulled into Pocatello in late summer 1978. I'd been looking forward to maximizing the distance between me and Hicksburg. Yet I couldn't fight the tears of fear and loneliness as I drove into the city and approached the campus of Idaho State University, home of the Bengals.

I was assigned a room with three seniors who'd roomed together for years. I was as welcome as Deep Throat to Richard Nixon or Bradley Manning to Barack Obama. I was sent packing before I unpacked.

A week and three dorm rooms later, I was frazzled down to my last, raw nerve. Trying to "fit in" while finding my way was posing quite the challenge. Nobody was particularly impressed that I'd been valedictorian of my high school graduating class of 37 individuals (N = 37). Or that I'd been quarterback of the unknown football team, shooting guard on the obscure basketball team, shortstop of the pathetic baseball team, and member of the National Honor Society. Out of the kiddie pool, into the reservoir known as Colonial Hall.

Not much later, the fun arrived. I spent most of the subsequent two years majoring in basketball and Women's Studies: shooting hoops as a walk-on for the major-college basketball team and studying women. I didn't exactly fail at either endeavor, although I received quite the up-bringing in humility. I was more intramural wannabe than Michael Jordan, more Don Quixote than Don Juan. Also, my extracurricular pursuits nearly cost me the aforementioned scholarship.

I had something of a fan club at one point during a long-lost basketball season. When the game would get out of hand—as it often did—my drunken brother and his drinking buddies would begin chanting on my behalf. I played a few minutes, and even earned a spot on the travel squad by the midpoint of the season. My total statistics for the single season I participated: 50 percent from the field (one basket in two attempts) and 50 percent from the free-throw line (ditto).

Immersed in an existential crisis typical for American teenagers unleashed into the world, I missed 42 consecutive days of every class during my second year on campus. This absence of intellectual curiosity presented something of a drag on my grade point average. The fact that my dorm room was the campus hot-spot for partying probably didn't help. Every weekend was a misguided fog of blue haze. I had the opposite of the Bill Clinton experience: I didn't smoke marijuana, but I inhaled.

From an academic perspective, the rare days I spent in class with my eyes open were disappointing on many levels. Having earned a solid F, I nonetheless received the only C of my collegiate career in my introductory macroeconomics course. At semester's end, I attempted to negotiate a higher grade from the instructor I was seeing for the fifth time: I showed up for all three in-class exams after I picked up the syllabus during the first class meeting. I thought I deserved at least a B. She wondered who I was, and kept smiling as she shook her head. Despite rarely making an appearance in her classroom, the class contributed to my contemporary definition of waste: a busload of economists goes over a cliff with an empty seat.

HOPE IS HOPELESS

Shortly after delivering a presentation in 2012, I received the following comment and question: "I have been listening and watching for ways to stimulate robust processes of social resilience. One idea is to talk about the difference between hope and hopium. Would you be willing to elaborate?"

I assume the reference to "social resilience" includes the desire to maintain industrial civilization, which I think is a terrible idea for many reasons. But perhaps I'm jumping to an incorrect conclusion.

In my 2011 book, *Walking Away from Empire*, I described hope as follows:

> I view hope as the left-brain product of love, analogous to democracy as the product of freedom, or liberty. Notably, Patrick Henry did not say, "Give me democracy or give me death." Like the rest of the founding fathers, Henry knew that freedom was primary to democracy; without the guiding light of freedom, or liberty, democracy breaks up on the shoals. Love keeps our left brain in check—that's the message of the world's religions. But our right-brain love creates the foundation for hope: love for nature, love for our children and grandchildren, love for each other. Without love to light the way, hope breaks up on the shoals.

Mind you, hope is not simply wishful thinking. And that's a problem, considering we're immersed in the ultimate "wishful thinking, something-for-nothing" culture. How else to explain books such as *The Secret*, which proclaims that happy thoughts will generate happy results, including personal wealth? How else to explain the prevalence of, and widespread acceptance of, casinos? And it's not just acceptance: it's adoration, if the boob tube and the local movie theater are to be believed. Not so long ago, gambling was frowned upon because, instead of adhering to a culture of an honest day's pay for an honest day's work, it reflects the expectation that a person can get something for nothing. No, hope is not wishful thinking.

And another thing: hope is not a consumer product. You can't walk into Wal-Mart and order up a carton of hope. Indeed, given the demise of cheap oil, there's unlikely to be a Wal-Mart—or any other large institution, for that matter—to walk into at all within a few years. Even if Wal-Mart, the federal government, or the University of Arizona somehow find a way to survive, we're going to have to generate our own hope, one person at a time. Just as an economic collapse happens one person at a time, so too must hope happen one person at a time.

Today, a few years later and after much time reflecting, I'm caught between my earlier description and the gradual merging of my view with the definition offered by Derrick Jensen in a 2006 essay in *Orion* magazine: "hope is a longing for a future condition over which you have no agency; it means you are essentially powerless."

In other words, my earlier description of hope is giving way to the notion of hope as wishful thinking, also known as hopium. I'm certainly not willing to give up, and I constantly encourage acts of resistance that will allow opportunities for the living planet to persist into the future. In so doing, I'm channeling iconoclastic Tucson author Edward Abbey: "Action is the antidote to despair."

Hopium is the drug to which we're addicted. It's the desire to have our problems solved by others, instead of by ourselves. It's why we keep electing politicians while knowing they won't keep their promises, but finding ourselves too fearful to give up the much-promised future of never-ending growth on a finite planet.

Knowing we cannot occupy this finite world without adverse consequences for humans or other animals, but afraid to face that truth, we turn away. We watch the television, go to the movies, gamble at casinos, play on Facebook, and pursue similar avenues of using up our precious time. Many Americans simultaneously applaud while the world burns as we take a flame-thrower to the planet. Nietzsche nailed it: "Hope is the most evil of evils, because it prolongs man's torment."

Finally, I've come to the conclusion that Nietzsche was right. I used to think hope differed from hopium, back when I had hope. Gradually, I've come to see hope and hopium as one. Let's get off the crack pipe, and onto reality. May Pandora release the final gift from her container (usually incorrectly referred to as her box).

This brief essay is not intended to suggest we abandon (1) resistance or (2) joy-filled lives. Life, including human life, is a gift. Let's live as if we appreciate the gift. Let's live as if we appreciate the others in our lives, human and otherwise. Let's live as if there is more to life than the treadmill onto which we were born.

Let's live.

Let's live now

Television anchor Edward R. Murrow is credited with this expression: "Just because your voice reaches halfway around the world doesn't mean you are wiser than when it reached only to the end of the bar." Murrow understood the power of television to misinform the masses. This strategy has worked brilliantly on every front, but none more pronounced than the all-important issue of global climate change. Seeking "balance" on the idiot box has meant that "both sides" of a one-sided issue have been presented, until it has finally become too late to address the crisis.

It's too late, at least for our species. We're already dead, and walking around only to save on funeral expenses.

Think of the deprivation we've brought to the world as we rape, pillage, and plunder Earth's glorious bounty for a few extra dollars with which to purchase toys that titillate and the high fructose corn syrup (aka "food") that's killing us.

Climate chaos is only a small part of the big story, and it will be addressed in a future essay because it is among the phenomena poised to cause our extinction within a single human generation. In addition to triggering climate chaos, we've initiated the Sixth Great Extinction, and we revel in its acceleration as one more sign of progress. Furthermore, we continue to ratchet up the madness of human-population overshoot on an overpopulated, overheated, increasingly lifeless planet. Environmental degradation proceeds apace as we gleefully trade in living soil for smart phones, clean air for fast computers, potable water for high-definition televisions, healthy food for industrial poison, contentment for exhilaration, decent human communities for the hierarchical death camps known as civilization, and life for death.

All the while, we take truth-tellers to task while looking to corrupt governments for leadership. Truth is treason in an empire of lies, as George Orwell poignantly wrote, so we don't protest governments that spy on their citizens and then kill them. The people, largely convinced they are consumers instead of citizens, keep seeking guidance from the television and nourishment from GMO-tainted faux food, all while seeking happiness from adrenaline instead of introspection.

My heart aches to the breaking point. Industrialized humans are destroying every aspect of the living planet with all the joy one would expect from homicidal maniacs. We don't think about what we're doing. If we did, we wouldn't. Or perhaps, driven by a culture of madness promoted by our contemporaries, we would.

I'm guilty, too, of course. Walking away from empire doesn't mean I've done enough to terminate the omnicidal set of living arrangements known as industrial civilization. Like others, I'm afraid of change, fearful to cash in my chips. But I'm afraid to stay, too. The thought of continuing to stare, alone, at the world of wounds induced by industrial civilization, causes the terror to rise in me. I'm afraid to let go of nature's bounty, as if it's mine to hold, by staying here. I'm afraid of what I'm missing by holding onto the relative comfort of my platinum-grade homestead.

Haunted by the wonder and beauty of nature and fully recognizing my efforts as insufficient, my bitterness nearly overshadows my overwhelming, debilitating sadness. How could I be so self-absorbed? What irreparable damage have I wrought by creating my lifeboat?

Curse your television. Then shoot it. It's not much, and it's too little, too late. But it's a therapeutic start to a much-needed revolution.

I feel nature slipping out of my grasp as we rush to destroy every species on Earth. With no decent solutions, my mind wanders between sadness and madness, between reality and the despair induced therein. Is it possible for a scientist to die from a broken heart?

What a way to go. We'd better start living, here and now.

Arts and minds

The overdeveloped left hemisphere of my brain tells me one thing. My emerging artistic side tells me another. But before we get to the core of the issue, a little personal history is warranted.

During my final decade in the classroom, I pushed an integrative agenda. Attempting to bridge C. P. Snow's eponymous "Two Cultures" in a manner consistent with Edward O. Wilson's *Consilience*, I required every student in each of my science courses to complete a significant piece of art or literature as a major part of the final grade. Naturally, the students hated the exercise and despised me, until the projects were complete and shared with the entire class, at which point the students unanimously agreed it was the most important activity they'd ever conducted in college. University administrators uniformly detested the exercise and just about everything else that happened in my classrooms. (And this was even before universities had become widely recognized as money-making scams reflective of this entire culture.) From a personal perspective, as I've pointed out before, the process of classroom-based integration caused me to lose my reason-driven way and venture deep into uncharted territory of the emotional life.

Therein lies the dilemma I face. Perhaps you face it, too. I know nary a scientist who actually understands and takes meaningful action on any of the following primary issues, much less all of them: human-population overshoot, destruction of non-industrial cultures, extinction of non-human species, peak oil, global climate change. I know plenty of scientists who teach some of these topics, I just don't know any who **understand** and **act** on them.

Conversely, I know several artists who understand the whole enchilada. Most of these people are marginalized by society because they are mere artists, so they have no voice. I'm not suggesting scientists have sufficient power to alter policy, or that any of these topics have politically viable solutions, but scientists can and have used reasonable argumentation to alter the views of a few thoughtful citizens. In general, and with a few notable, high-profile exceptions, artists have been less effective. Perhaps being ignored and marginalized allows artists to reach acceptance about imperial decline and other matters of significance.

But back to me—my favorite subject, after all—and my internal struggle. My heart keeps informing me, with its never-ending screams into my inner ears, that we must terminate this set of living arrangements before it kills us all. My brain, on the other hand, tells me it's too late: Near-term extinction is locked in because of Fukushima (times 400 and change), climate chaos, and environmental decay. All three paths of horror indicate our species has a few decades at most. I know a little about these three phenomena, but there are doubtless others. And I'm certainly not depending on the people who claim to be in charge because I know they lost control when global oil peaked, even though they keep juggling chickens and chain saws in an effort to distract the masses.

In light of this overwhelming onslaught of horrifying information, my heart tells me to seize the day, go with the flow, and a few other tattered clichés. It tells me to more fully immerse myself in nature and humanity, to breathe deeply and laugh often, to throw off the shackles of mitigating for economic collapse in this location even if it means going down with the ship of empire. Or maybe that's the limbic part of my brain rising to the fore, not my heart. My obnoxiously contrarian brain—the cognitive part to which I'm particularly well-tuned—chimes in with unwelcome advice aimed at convincing people of our dire straits, as if I've made even a minor difference, while of course trying to destroy this irredeemably corrupt system.

In addition to my overdeveloped science side, I've no doubt there are other contributors to my inability to lean toward heartfelt intuition. Five decades of cultural programming come immediately to mind.

Integrating these two disparate approaches seems impossible, although I didn't see it that way when I was asking students to do it. Perhaps that's why I can't answer this question: How does one simultaneously follow one's heart and one's brain when they point in opposite directions?

This internal struggle feels like a battle for my non-existent soul. That reason rules, for now, leaves my heart in shards. The inability to integrate myself, to become fully human, leaves me with heartache that is irreconcilable with becoming fully human. Perhaps it's even lethal. After all, human survival requires a heart and a brain.

Falling in love again
When I was young, I fell in the love with the girl next door. Well, maybe it wasn't love. But she was lovely and it felt like love, to my young heart. It wasn't about sex, although she was sexy. Color me smitten.

Fast-forward a few years, and I fall again. I'm older, perhaps more mature, maybe even wiser. But I fall just as hard. She's seductive, and I'm seduced. This time, it sticks for a long while. This time, she's alluring, attractive, dream-like, sexy, desired by every man I know. She plays hard to get, but I catch her and the dream she represents. For decades, I switch to cruise control, taking for granted the dream I've corralled. For decades, she's always there for me, and me for her. Thinking we're working hard, we entertain often, buy the expected baubles, and travel when we want.

It's coming apart now. She's familiar with the thoughts of Marcus Aurelius, which makes her afraid of the future: "Look back over the past, with its changing empires that rose and fell, and you can foresee the future, too." I'm excited about the future, and I can no longer live in the past. I've done the entire Kübler-Ross cycle of grief, slipping back-and-forth as frequently as I once dined with her.

My denial was profound. How could it be over? We're perfect for each other. We've never really known another, not like this. Please, tell me it's just a phase.

My anger was brief and deep. Sometimes I look back on those days through my Buddhism-inspired lens, aghast I could have been so ridiculous. It was nobody's fault, really. We grow. Sometimes we grow together. Sometimes we grow apart.

I still bargain, if only in my mind. What about shorter showers or, better yet, longer showers together? Surely we can merely cut back a little on our excesses, and we'll be fine. I'm willing to compromise. But of course I know better. There's no putting the air back in these shredded tires.

Depression visits, too. Trading in the comforts of familiarity for a new and different set of experiences is difficult at my advanced age. Dark nights alone at the mud hut drive me to tears. Tears come on sunny days, too, as I lean against the stem of a big cottonwood tree or lie on the ground near the river, reduced to a trickle by the insults of industry.

Acceptance came late, and skips away too often. But I'm building a new relationship now, one based on trust and mutual respect. It's not about the sex, though she's sexy. It's about love, and she's lovely. She's kind, playful, and passionate. She doesn't judge me, though my inadequacies are legion. She's courageous and strong, in sharp contrast to my ever-present fear and fragility. I'm a tree-hugging dirt worshiper, and she likes to play in the dirt; when I'm feeling particularly flirtatious, I refer to her as my dirty girl. She accommodates my whimsy, and I love hers. I can scarcely believe she's the same one I knew, and left, so many years ago. This time, I'll not let go. I want to spend my remaining days with her.

After constantly taking from others and occasionally giving to me, Athena—the goddess of civilization—is dead to me. I miss her now and then, but I'm back with Nature now. Although I was slow to the realization, Nature provides all I need, and all I've ever needed. Color me smitten, yet again.

Next up: Into the wild?

American essayist Norman Cousins wrote: "Death is not the greatest loss in life. The greatest loss is what dies inside us while we live."

Personally, I've never been content sitting still, surviving for survival's sake. Evidence is found in the roller coaster of my academic career, which was marked by significant change every few years. My scholarship, teaching, and service were characterized by unpredictable, nonlinear, seemingly chaotic swings from one topic to another. The adventure of new experiences always trumped the security of the bricks-on-a-pile approach revered in the ivory tower. A primary point I made in every course I taught: It's always more difficult to do the right thing than to do the wrong thing. In fact, you can usually tell the right direction simply by comparing the difficulty of the choices you face.

For working outside the mainstream in a dysfunctional system, I paid in expected ways, including financially. But I benefitted in ways I could not have expected and still cannot fully describe. A rich life comes from taking risks, and the risks range from physical to emotional. I've had a rich life.

Most recently, I've thrown my heart, soul, and every last dime into the mud hut. I suspect it's the consummate lifeboat, and it illustrates how an improperly talented but reasonably thoughtful person can develop a durable set of living arrangements. And in the desert, no less. If we can make it work here, if only for the very few more years before habitat for humans fades into oblivion, I suspect it can work in just about any habitable place on this blue dot.

The response from the masses: I'm insane. I suppose this should have been expected from a culture characterized by sheer insanity. As with nearly everybody in this culture, I was born into captivity. I spent most of my life in the zoo that is contemporary culture, drinking and feeding at the troughs of indulgence and denial and playing with toys that substitute for reality (albeit poorly). To a great extent, I'm still in the zoo, still immersed in the culture of make believe.

I'm attempting to pursue, and encourage, agrarian anarchy in the small valley I occupy. We're at the edge of empire, but we're still part of the American Empire. David Graeber explains the general idea in the analysis of the Occupy movement he wrote for *Al-Jazeera* in November 2011:

The easiest way to explain anarchism is to say that it is a political movement that aims to bring about a genuinely free society—that is, one where humans only enter those kinds of relations with one another that would not have to be enforced by the constant threat of violence. History has shown that vast inequalities of wealth, institutions like slavery, debt peonage or wage labour, can only exist if backed up by armies, prisons, and police. Anarchists wish to see human relations that would not have to be backed up by armies, prisons and police. Anarchism envisions a society based on equality and solidarity, which could exist solely on the free consent of participants.

Fiery desert anarchist Edward Abbey put his own spin on the notion of anarchy, which was the subject of his master's degree at the University of New Mexico: "Anarchism is not a romantic fable but the hardheaded realization, based on five thousand years of experience, that we cannot entrust the management of our lives to kings, priests, politicians, generals, and county commissioners."

Graeber's description offers a worthy ideal for civil society. Serious pursuit of this ideal would go a long way toward allowing us to regain our humanity. Whether it goes far enough depends on the human. I'm wondering if living on the edge is good enough for me, whether instead I should leap from the edge into the abyss of the uncivilized.

There is another challenge, perhaps as great and certainly as important as the one I've undertaken here at the mud hut: making it work on the road, thus engendering full expression of the human animal. Imagine a minimalist approach to the road and to the wilds surrounding the road. Imagine the exhilaration of abandoning a lifeboat to swim in frigid, shark-filled waters. Imagine the wonder of full immersion into the world, surrounded by every element of the human condition and every element of nature.

Ultimately, perhaps shortly before our own near-term extinction, full immersion into the world is exactly where we're headed. I could show the way into tribalism beyond civilization, as I've shown the way by exiting empire. And although I suspect the number of followers would be similarly disappointing, I would be taking this step for myself, not for others, as is the case now.

Nature calls. She calls all of us, though most of us have managed to plug our ears to her siren song. For a few, though, the temptation is supreme from the ultimate temptress. She's kind, playful, passionate, courageous, strong, and whimsical. Can I pursue her? Can I capture her spirit, as she has captured my heart? Can I find the human animal within me before I breathe my last breath? Nature, as always, is amorally indifferent to my (therefore unrequited) love. But touching her and, more importantly, having her touch me, seems a one-way street: Once ensconced in her embrace, there's no going back.

At this point in the age of industry, perhaps any attempt to venture into the wild is pure fantasy. Culture certainly suggests as much, while indicating that a step away from my current living arrangements is one large step on the short path to a bygone era. Bygone for a reason, says culture: There's no going back to nature. That's just crazy talk.

A few paragraphs earlier, commenting on my new love, I wrote, "Nature provides all I need, and all I've ever needed." If I believe myself, shouldn't I attempt to prove it? Or, to put the scientific spin on it, shouldn't I attempt to disprove it?

Can I find my way into a world that is brave and new and as old as humanity? More importantly, should I?

Taking a large step away from civilization will almost certainly shorten my life. As I've pointed out many times, (1) birth is lethal and (2) some things are worth dying for. Whereas, in the spirit of the musical *Eagles*, I've no intention of becoming yet another starry-eyed Messiah destined for a violent farewell, neither am I interested in a sedate, risk-free life. Like most people, I'm trying to find the line Cousins inferred, the line between living outside—in the world—and dying inside. And, of course, doing the right thing, regardless of the inherent risks and challenges.

THE KNIFE AND THE NUN

I started exchanging physical labor for fiat currency when I was about 12 years old. Nine-month stints spent within indoctrination facilities were interrupted by summers spent clearing fields of woody debris: Small landowners converted forests to fields and other youngsters and I tossed sticks onto a "low-boy" trailer pulled by a slow-moving tractor. At the end of the day, my mom wouldn't let me into the house until she sprayed off the first few layers of dirt with a hose. My first job was called, "picking sticks." It was miserable work for little pay.

A couple years later, when I was stronger, I moved up the small-town ladder. Former forests had become fields of alfalfa, and I bucked bales onto a trailer pulled by a slow-moving tractor. A short ride later, we stacked the bales in the barn. The per-hour pay of $2.50 represented a modest improvement over my previous employment. Equally importantly, I felt more like a man and less like a boy when I took responsibility for my own shower at the end of the work day.

Beyond sticks and bales

A few odd jobs later I landed the premier employment opportunity for an 18-year-old athlete living in a small town in the interior western United States. On 1 July 1978 I secured the title of Fire Control Aide I for the Idaho Department of

Lands. I wore the uniform of the era: leather work boots, a long-sleeved cotton shirt, blue jeans and a Bowie knife on my belt (the latter for easy access to cut a fire hose).

Naturally, this gig was strictly for summer. I was headed for college and, unlike the majority of today's youngsters, I was prepared for college, at least with respect to knowledge and work ethic. I was, of course, socially, emotionally, and psychologically naive. But I was certain the road out of a life of labor in Hicksville went through college.

Along with another neophyte smokechaser named Bill, I was driven by our supervisor to the remote field camp where we were stationed. Neither of us possessed a vehicle—I bought my own first car a few years later—so we were relegated to bumming a ride with anybody headed in the right direction. Since that direction included only the barest semblance of civilization, there wasn't much traffic. On that first day of employment, our supervisor spent considerable time teaching us how to read a map along the route. Along the way, he hammered into us the importance of introducing ourselves to our few neighbors as we completed the "make-work" tasks developed specifically to enhance the physical condition of the young men hired to fight wildfires. At the time, all Fire Control Aides working for the Idaho Department of Lands were men, and a primary goal of supervisors was to keep the men busy with strenuous physical labor, hence in fine physical condition, lest boredom creep in and invoke mischief.

Bill hailed from the city and he seemed even more inept than me so, assuming control as a control freak would, I took the wheel. The seat belts were buried beneath the ancient, recalcitrant seats, so we didn't bother with them. The wipers swept the windshield erratically and only when I decelerated. The defroster didn't defrost. And every puddle in the pock-marked gravel road shot through the floor boards. Trying to cure these three ills simultaneously with a roll of paper towels led to the expected conclusion. Right before the lights went out, I recall the road coming up to meet my face.

So much for assuming control of the situation.

Now what?

Thrown from the vehicle, I awoke flat on my back and opened my eyes to utter darkness. "That's not right," I thought. I closed my eyes, rubbed them with my fingers, and opened them again. Cleared of the blood that had pooled in my eye sockets, my eyes found the clouds. I blinked into the falling rain. Problem solved.

Turning my head allowed me to see a swath of detritus between me and the jeep, now firmly lodged against a pine tree, albeit surprisingly resting on four wheels. Two shovels, two canteens, a hose reel, and two Pulaskis—the famous fire-fighting tool wielded by my grandfather and father before me—comprised a 10-foot-wide strip about a hundred feet from me to the tree.

Bringing myself to a standing position proved challenging. I had no feeling in my left leg below my hip. Yet again I thought, "that's not right." My two-sizes-too-small brain was stuck on obvious, with only three words at my disposal.

I remembered my traveling companion, and shouted his name a few times. Bill finally responded, and seemed no worse for wear. He wasn't limping, and his head was bleeding slightly less than mine. Next up: find a ride to town.

Within a matter of minutes, a pickup truck appeared on the scene. The rancher rolled down his window and silently looked us over. I asked for a ride to the nearest hospital, and he invited us onto the bench seat.

Bill propped up his head—now I noticed it wasn't staying upright unless he held it up—and introduced us: "I'm Bill, and this is Guy. We're Fire Control Aides with the Idaho Department of Lands." The uppercase letters in our shared title were obvious. I was proud of the title, too.

The man behind the wheel responded, "I'm Jack Green."

Rinse and repeat

Lacking feeling in my left leg, I asked Jack to take us to the nearest hospital. He pointed out that the nearest hospital was run by nuns in Cottonwood. I said that'd be fine. He recommended spending the extra half hour to drive to the hospital in Grangeville. I insisted to the contrary, my leg causing concern I was unable or unwilling to articulate while Bill and I passed the roll of paper towels back and forth to swab our bleeding foreheads.

Yet again, Bill pushed his head upright on his neck and introduced us, his voice tinged with pride: "I'm Bill, and this is Guy. We're Fire Control Aides with the Idaho Department of Lands."

Jack responded, "I'm Jack Green."

Immersed in self-pity, I stared out the passenger-side window at the rain-soaked countryside. Every few minutes I'd wrest the roll of paper towels from Bill, peel off the outer layer or two, and apply it with all the pressure I could muster to my lacerated forehead. His own head unsupported by his hands and the roll of paper towels, Bill's head would then fall onto his shoulder. As if for the first time, he'd push his head upright on his neck and introduce us, his voice tinged with pride: "I'm Bill, and this is Guy. We're Fire Control Aides with the Idaho Department of Lands."

Ever the gentleman, Jack would respond, "I'm Jack Green."

A few dozen repetitions of this routine left me with one remaining nerve, and it was raw and exposed. Every time Bill introduced us, I yelled at him to shut up. The rancher, cool as the falling rain, never failed to introduce himself in the same level tone.

There's no way I was riding an extra 30 minutes with these two fools. I didn't know many Catholics, but I wasn't afraid of nuns. We'll take the first stop, please.

About my leg

Covered with blankets but still shivering from shock shortly after landing bottom-side up on a gurney, I was congratulating myself for making it this far. I was still worried about my numb left leg, but I could no longer hear Bill's endless identical introductions, and the hospital didn't seem so bad. It probably helped that I'd had no prior experience with hospitals. Not as a patient, in any event.

Had I been fully cognizant, the veritable absence of activity would have served as a warning beyond the one offered by Jack Green. Not only was I not fully cognizant, I was self-absorbed, as usual, and also busily bargaining with the Christian god I thought I'd abandoned a few years earlier. Blood was pouring out my forehead, I was shaking like a hummingbird in hailstorm, and my left leg was dead.

Enter the nun. She came in behind me, removed the blankets to expose my naked backside, and promptly removed the blade of the Bowie knife previously embedded into my left cheek. The one characterized by the large muscle known as gluteus maximus. The feeling returned in my left leg quite abruptly. My leg afire in pain, the nun waves the broken blade before my eyes and asks, "Is this yours?"

My immediate thought: Please put it back.

My second thought: I should've listened to Jack Green about the hospitals.

The latter thought was reinforced several times during the subsequent 24 hours. For example, the ER doctor was stitching up my forehead while the nun was pouring Novocain into the new hole in my left butt cheek. Each burning drop of Novocain caused my head to jerk into the man with the needle, thus assisting the mostly incompetent doc with the suturing process. Far more importantly was Bill's broken neck, which the hospital failed to diagnose. I can only imagine how much money I cost the Idaho Department of Lands when Bill and his family sued the organization. Then, as now, I had the good fortune of having nothing for which to sue.

Silver lining

As always, I'm Mr. Silver Lining. Shortly after the voluminous reports were complete, every vehicle under the care of the Idaho Department of Lands sported a roll-bar. In this most litigious of societies, my actions induced the organization to protect against idiocy by protecting idiots. We progressives call this progress.

And there's a bit more, although it's as personal as this self-indulgent essay. If you've made it this far, there's still time to avert the worst.

I learned a lesson about immortality. I don't have it.

I learned a lesson about control. I don't have it, either.

I learned a lesson about hubris. Suddenly, I had less. By now, I have considerably less than I did in 1978.

SPREADING THE HORROR

I'm pretty sure you know the drill. You pose the scenario and ask the hypothetical questions: *There's an asteroid headed for Earth. We know exactly when it will strike, and it will kill all humans. Do you want to know if it will strike? If so, do you want to know when it will strike?*

I know of no poll results, but I've asked the question a few times. Some people want to know everything. Others don't want to know anything.

Ignorance is bliss?

People who want to know when the asteroid will strike cannot fathom that people don't want to know. People who don't want to know the asteroid is headed our way cannot fathom why anybody would want to know. Obviously, I'm in the former camp, spreading the news like Nutella on a croissant, as if people not only care about knowledge, but want to lap it up.

In fact, it's inconceivable to me that people don't want to know. I want to stare, unblinking, when the asteroid strikes. I want to peer into the abyss of my mortality, eyes wide open, knowing the exact moment I will depart this mortal coil. Not in the name of courage, but curiosity.

I have begun using this scenario and the attendant hypothetical questions to introduce my presentations. (As an aside, the potential for speaking tours comes up quite frequently for me. Then, as prospective hosts fully understand the messages I'll be transmitting, they fade away, often with no explanation and no response to my repeated messages.) Back to the point: If I used the hypothetical questions in my introduction, it would allow participants an opportunity to leave the premises before they hear the worst of it. They'd be out a few minutes of time, but they'd save some time and they'd depart relatively free of angst. Ignorance is bliss, especially with respect to challenging social issues, and who am I to rob people of their bliss?

Like the ninth person to arrive at a party for eight, I missed "fitting in" only by a smidgen. If I'm angry because I'm late to the party, you get to bear the brunt of my anger by reading about it here. My only defense is the line that's become a bumper-sticker cliché: If you're not outraged, you're not paying attention.

For me, not knowing is unbearable. But knowing is a great burden, too. And while I'm expecting an asteroid oddly shaped like climate chaos, we'll probably get hit by a meteor.

If I did not know about the horrors of empire, I would still be teaching at a university. I would still be drawing a large paycheck doing the work I love and interacting with idealistic young people. I would have the respect and admiration of civilized people, including my parents and siblings.

If I did not know about the horrors of climate change, I would be content with my path in life. I would be living large, sleeping well, and enjoying the contentment of a life well lived. Rarely would I attract animus from across the sociopolitical spectrum. Angst would lie in abeyance, along with threats on my life.

What a boring existence that would be. For better and worse, I'm stuck with the current adventure: the adventure of a lifetime until the adventure ends, along with the life.

There are no second chances, no opportunities to undo what's been done. At the level of individuals, we refer to poor choices as stupidity (when others are making the choices) or tragedy (when it's us). At the level of our ill-fated species, we refer to the myriad poor choices as progress. As nearly as I can distinguish, when faced with the proverbial fork in the road, we've taken the wrong turn at each and every opportunity. And yet we keep plugging along, claiming we're sapient progressives. A few among us claim to be conservatives, but we're conserving only this omnicidal way of life. Until we can't.

We're committing suicide at the level of our entire species, and too many other species to correctly tally. All that's left is more excuses in an endless string of excuses from the architects and marketers of industrial civilization. I won't hold my breath for their long-overdue apologies.

I'm not suggesting all the bliss of ignorance is inexplicable. The corporate governments of the world have been following the playbook of former CIA director William Casey since long before he uttered these words in 1981: "We'll know our disinformation program is complete when everything the American public believes is false." It's working great, as indicated by the one-third of Americans who would accept cavity searches in exchange for the privilege of flying commercial airlines, among many other such anecdotes.

An empire in decline requires obedience at home, and it helps if the populace remains purposefully ignorant. At a weekly White House meeting dubbed "Terror Tuesdays," the drone-bomber-in-chief decides who will die without a whiff of due process, transparency, or oversight (and he has plenty of video-game operators forgoing their consciences to pull the trigger). Democratic National Committee chair Debbie Wasserman Schultz claimed in October 2012 that she had never heard of Obama's infamous "kill list," thus branding herself either a liar or stunningly ignorant (if she's lying, she has plenty of company in the halls of our governing bodies).

Obama has given himself power over all communication systems in the country, and he can wiretap, indefinitely detain, and kill any of us on a whim, thereby indicating how meaningless is the Bill of Rights. In addition, he's constantly seeking more power (including pre-emptive prosecution, in case he believes you're thinking about committing a crime). Obama's brand of evil, which includes dictatorial assassinations and ongoing destruction of the Constitution and the Bill of Rights, is exceeded only by the audacity and willful ignorance of his supporters.

Obedience is mandatory

As if he could peer into the future, American author Henry David Thoreau is credited with the expression: "Disobedience is the true foundation of liberty. The obedient must be slaves."

I've written and spoken often about the requirements for maintaining an empire, particularly an empire in decline: obedience at home, oppression abroad, and wholesale destruction of the living planet. I've written numerous essays about the latter two phenomena. Although I've spoken about a few examples concerning obedience at home, I've not previously focused on the topic with a single essay.

Herein I present a few recent examples of obedience at home. This essay is hardly comprehensive, and the hits keep coming. But it's a minor start to a major issue. I'm certain many more examples will appear—though not to the typical, purposely ignorant American—until American Empire finally sinks to the bottom of the cesspool in which it is mired.

I focus on the Obama administration because it is the most recent and also the most horrific example of imperialism. I refuse to play the game currently popular among Democrats in which Obama is compared to Mitt Romney or John McCain. Obama has a record as president, and Romney and McCain don't. I cannot imagine a worse president than Obama, although that's what I thought about his predecessor, too. I'm hardly the only person to refer to Obama as the worst president ever. Full disclosure: When I was registered to vote, I was a lifelong Democrat.

When he was in the Oval Office, I thought Ronald Reagan was the worst president ever. But I still recall thinking, when Reagan was shot, that it could be worse: We could have his vice president, ex-director of the Central Intelligence Agency (CIA) George Herbert Walker Bush, as president. A few days shy of eight years later, we did. Then along came Slick Willy, who slyly managed to outflank his predecessor and the opposing party on several significant issues. In every case, Bill Clinton outflanked the opposition by moving further to the political right. Just when I thought it couldn't get any worse, George W. Bush was selected. Twice. And then, he was replaced by somebody even worse. In my voting lifetime, each neo-conservative U.S.

president has been replaced by a worse version. And lest you believe otherwise, our two-party, one-ideology system of governance is working brilliantly. It's not working for us, but that's never been the plan.

Within my lifetime, Democrats have shifted far to the right, thus co-opting the ideas of the Grand Old Party. The latter party is effectively gone, serving only to make the Democrats seem sane by comparison. Obama and the Democrats can get away with every imaginable abuse—and many abuses I could not have imagined until they occurred—simply by using the Republicans as cover. The corporate media are fully engaged in the cover-up, as pointed out in the 21 March 2013 issue of *Harper's* magazine: "Barack Obama... never stops serving the ruling class, yet the mainstream media, from right to left, continues to pretend that he's some sort of reincarnation of Franklin D. Roosevelt, fully committed to the downtrodden and deeply hostile to the privileged and the rich."

Obama's corporate government is doing the bidding of the corporations. The corporate media aids and abets the enemies of the people. As Noam Chomsky points out, "any dictator would admire the uniformity and obedience of the U.S. media." The American people, fully convinced they are consumers instead of citizens, capitulate to their masters. The unseen bars keep the people enslaved.

Obama seeks cradle-to-grave power to rule over Americans, with examples that are breathtaking in their number and scope. He is responsible for torture, according to a two-year independent investigation by the Constitution Project released 16 April 2013. Obama's Department of Justice has brought charges against six whistle-blowers under the Espionage Act of 1917, a number that exceeds every previous administration combined. Indeed, he destroys whistle-blowers with a hateful vengeance, with a recent example focusing on a man who tried to reduce government waste. In the Orwellian style for which he has become infamous, Obama now requires his staff and the complicit media to refer to whistle-blowers as "leakers." His vision of the United States is termed "Obama's wiretap America" in the 8 May 2013 issue of *Salon*, although it's merely an extension of policies in place since at least 2001, according to an 11 May 2006 story in *USA Today*. Even before then, the National Security Agency (NSA) had a back door built into Windows software. Obama's government gives AT&T and other telecommunications companies secret immunity from wiretap laws. In fact, officials in his administration have authorized a new government program involving the interception of communications on Internet service providers, as well as to record every single telephone conversation (as reported in the *Guardian* as recently at 6 June 2013). The same day, the *Washington Post* reported that one of George W. Bush's legacies, continued by Obama, is a collaboration between U.S. spy agencies and Microsoft, Yahoo, Google, Facebook, PalTalk, AOL, Skype, YouTube, and Apple. Oh, and Obama's Internal Revenue Service could be, and probably is, reading your email without a warrant. These invasions of privacy in the name of security—an overview of the "best" articles on this worst of horrors was offered by ProPublica in June 2013—are merely warm-up acts for the massive NSA data collection and analysis center under construction in Utah which, according to former NSA official William Binney, puts us very near "a turnkey totalitarian state." Binney was a crypto-mathematician largely responsible for automating the agency's worldwide eavesdropping network until he left the agency in 2001.

All of this probably is fine with most Americans. It's been a long, relatively gradual road to this point. Most American citizens favor being spied upon, according to a poll conducted 6-9 June 2013 by the Pew Research Center and the *Washington Post*. Most Americans also favor imprisoning terrorist suspects even without evidence to convict, according to a Rasmussen poll conducted in April 2013. And we're busily looking the other way as the NSA uses a bogus, secret interpretation of the Patriot Act to get away with recording millions of telephone calls and retaining every email message for an indeterminate length of time. Fortunately for them and all of us law-abiding citizens, Obama refuses to close the prison at Guantanamo Bay—yet another in an endless string of broken campaign promises—and instead has approved major upgrades.

And, lest we ever forget, I'm here to remind you what George W. Bush and his cabal of evil-doers proclaimed: Those terrorists hate us for our freedoms.

Many people more informed than I have argued that the Central Intelligence Agency (CIA) is running the show, and has been doing so at least as far back as 22 November 1963. One needn't get into the big picture to point out that the CIA's mission, with respect to data, is "collect everything and hang onto it forever." The CIA admits to using broadcast news to manipulate the American citizenry as far back as 1954. The good-guy/bad-guy story of Al Qaeda is a classic example of an organization founded by the CIA in 1998, and then demonized by the CIA and other government entities.

Rather than the CIA running the show, maybe the big banks have been in charge, at least since the 1990s.

According to the 29 December 2012 issue of the *Guardian*, the brutal crackdown on Occupy was coordinated by the big banks. Indeed, a compelling case can be made that JP Morgan Chase runs the whole show, since the Federal Reserve Bank and JP Morgan Chase appear to be the same entity, with a shared vault exposed by investigate reporters at the website Zero Hedge (zerohedge.com).

Rather than the CIA or the big banks running the show, maybe it's the tyranny of oligarchy. Consider the revolving doors between the federal government and corporations. A recent example has former CIA head and four-star Army General David Petraeus joining buyout firm KKR & Co. L.P. (formerly known as Kohlberg Kravis Roberts & Co.), one of the world's largest private equity firms.

Not surprisingly, the corporate media is barely making a peep as Obama's corporate government continues to practice socialism for the rich and capitalism for the poor. Why do you think a homeless man gets a 15-year sentence for stealing a few dollars whereas a CEO receives a 3-year sentence for stealing $3 billion? Why do you think local police officers work for Exxon after a spill? Why do you think the Fifth Amendment no longer exists as a functioning law of the land?

Obama's corporate government flaunts the illegal acquisition of information as he launches a war on journalism, according to recent reporting by the *Guardian* and *Slate*. Too little, too late, the corporate media express outrage long after they acquiesced to fascism. A recent example is the *New York Times* calling for the citizenry to trust the official government story on the Boston bombing or be proclaimed insane.

Contrary to popular belief in the neoconservative blogosphere, Obama is not coming for your guns. The federal government has way more artillery than the citizenry could possibly muster, and it is no longer able to cover up huge purchases of ammunition. Writing for the 11 April 2013 issue of *Guardian*, Glenn Greenwald exposes Obama's lies about drones: (1) The Obama administration often has no idea who they are killing; (2) Whistle-blowers are vital for transparency and accountability, which is precisely why the Obama administration is waging a war on them; and (3) Secrecy ensures both government lies and abuses of power. A month after Greenwald's piece appeared, Obama finally admitted his drones killed four Americans. That's why Obama and his government don't care about your guns: They have more firepower than you.

The feds don't need your guns, but they're broke, so they need your money. Already, a confiscation scheme is planned for the United Kingdom and the U.S. according to Ellen Brown, attorney and president of the Public Banking Institute, in her 28 March 2013 essay at *Counterpunch*. Unfortunately for the government, it's getting a little late to extract fiat currency from most Americans. In a closely related issue, the criminalization of political dissent is complete in America.

It's difficult for me to imagine a more passive citizenry than the one that currently resides in the American empire. Surely Thoreau would be stunned.

THEATER OF THE ABSURD

En route to Tucson for a two-day visit, I retrieved my mail from the local post office. Included was one of the few Christmas/New Year letters to appear in 2012. Apparently you have to write them to receive them, and in this case it was a form letter from a long-time friend and colleague. The opening line took me aback: "Especially considering the political strife and random unexplainable (sic) violence of the past year, we find ourselves feeling incredibly blessed..."

Wow. Apparently this particular professor hasn't been paying attention to the news. Or perhaps she is plagued by the sentiments of James Baldwin, the American novelist, essayist, playwright, poet, and social critic: "Precisely at the point when you begin to develop a conscience you must find yourself at war with society." Being at war with society is a tough sell for a university professor embedded within and dependent upon the current version of society. After all, this is the society that brings her blessings, courtesy of American Empire.

Fitting in with absurdity

Thinking of my friend and her predicament brings to mind Loren Eiseley, the American anthropologist, educator, philosopher, and natural science writer. Because of Eiseley's intense and poetic writing style, and his focus on nature and cosmology, he was not accepted or understood by most of his colleagues. "You," a friend told him, "are a freak, you know. A God-damned freak, and life is never going to be easy for you. You like scholarship, but the scholars, some of them, anyhow, are not going to like you because you don't stay in the hole where God supposedly put you. You keep sticking your head out and looking around. In a university that's inadvisable."

If being at war with society is a tough sell for a university professor, you can only imagine how difficult is the challenge of being at war with the very university writing the paychecks. (As an aside, I need not imagine the challenge. I've lived it.)

The violence is "random, unexplainable" only if you've been living under a rock for a very long time. The violence visited upon countries in the Middle East and northern Africa by the current war criminal in the Oval Office—fully supported by my long-time friend—is all about the Carter Doctrine (i.e., the world is our oilster). Even the mainstream media have outed Obama as a war criminal, but he doesn't care enough to change policy (and there's no need, with supporters like my friend backing his every vile maneuver).

I don't know if my friend's car sports the "Obama for Peace" bumper sticker seemingly required for self-proclaimed liberals in this country. As with anybody who believes Obama is promoting peace, she'd better not poll the citizens of Iraq, Afghanistan, Libya, Pakistan, Yemen, and Somalia (and doubtless other countries bombed by the current commander in chief).

Even Obama's Secretary of Defense, Republican Senator Chuck Hagel, once admitted the truth to law students: "People say we're not fighting for oil. Of course we are. They talk about America's national interest. What the hell do you think they're talking about? We're not there for figs."

The line echoes in my head all the way to Tucson: "political strife and random unexplainable violence." It's as if I've seen a twenty-car pile-up on the Interstate highway. There's blood on the Christmas gifts. But in this case, the blood isn't merely on the packages. It's on our hands. Looking away, as my friend chooses, doesn't make the blood go away.

Maybe, instead of looking at the violence our military carries overseas, my friend was referring to the lack of violence she perceives here in the homeland. Unable to wrap her mind around the "obedience at home" mentality required by police state America, perhaps she subconsciously replaces contemporary evidence with an idyllic image from her youth. The image was incorrect then, too, but she was too young to understand America as a rapacious empire. At this point, she's old enough to know better. If she lived in Houston or Miami, her cries to support the troops would be overwhelmed by the gunfire and rotor blades as U.S. military helicopters conduct drills. Hell, even her beloved *New York Times* asks the question on 16 January 2013: Who Says You Can Kill Americans, Mr. President?

The line ricochets in my skull: "political strife and random unexplainable violence." Like most professors, she's a cheerleader for empire, unable to question the costs of imperialism. In financial terms alone, these costs run between $22 billion and $250 billion annually (maybe more). But we're so deeply in debt we'll never climb out, even if we believe the fiction of U.S. debt in the few tens of trillions of dollars.

But money is the least of the costs. After all, we simply print the world's reserve currency in the greatest Ponzi scheme of all time. The truly significant costs include the U.S. occupation of Africa, which will tally 35 nations later this year. Well, 35 the Department of Defense admits to occupying. Only five years after AFRICOM was established, the occupation of Africa is complete.

Obama's drone wars are sold to a willing adoring citizenry under the guise of minimizing American deaths because they spare sending our troops into combat. Collateral damage from the drones accounts for 49 out of 50 kills in Pakistan, but Americans can't be bothered with the details. Never mind the Orwellian double-speak from the President himself: "there is no country on earth that would tolerate missiles raining down on its citizens from outside its borders."

Meanwhile, lawyers in the U.S. Department of Justice (sic) claim drone targets receive due process, but they won't say how. And Americans simply don't want to know. "Liberals" such as my friend and purported scholar keep listening to NPR (National Propaganda Radio) as it leads the cheers for imperialism.

I thought good news was on the way when I read a headline: "The First Prison Sentence Related to Gitmo Torture..." Then I finished reading the headline, and the story. Sickeningly, the first person sentenced for torture at Guantanamo Bay was ex-CIA officer John C. Kiriakoua, a whistle-blower hunted down by the Obama administration because he spoke out against torture at the facility Obama promised to close throughout his initial campaign, and several times after he took office. In January 2013, Kiriakoua was sentenced to 30 months in prison.

At this point, any reasonably literate person can see the whole story as it unfolds in slow motion. In this country, we initiate terrorism to create terrorists to overthrow governments. And then, the president moves to make war on terror permanent. It goes around and around, the tail chasing the dog and Americans seeking every opportunity to look away. A movie was created about it, nearly four decades ago, called *Three Days of the Condor*.

My penalty for the intellectually torturous three-hour drive was landing in Tucson for two days. Any city, epitomized by the one that imports its water from more than 300 miles across the desert—uphill, no less—drives me further down the path of crazy. It doesn't help that my friends and colleagues in the Old Pueblo find themselves "incredibly blessed" (aka willingly blind) or that they find me a "God-damned freak" (maybe they're not so blind, after all). Given a choice, I wish I could un-see most of what I see.

Americans love money

In a letter to Ernest de Chabrol dated 9 June 1831, Alexis de Tocqueville wrote: "As one digs deeper into the national character of the Americans, one sees that they have sought the value of everything in this world only in the answer to this single question: how much money will it bring in?"

Nearly two hundred years later, de Tocqueville has been vindicated not only as a superb social critic but also as a forecaster. Knowing nothing about de Tocqueville, the ten-year-old son of a friend put his own spin on recent history: "Mom, I think people value Father Time more than they value Mother Earth." His words sting me like freezing rain, squeezing tears from the corners of my eyes. There's nothing new there for me, except the perspective of youth:

I often weep when I think about the hellishly overheated world we're leaving him and his young friends. We're destroying this world in large part because we care more about chasing fiat currency than we care about the living planet and its occupants.

Although it seems unlikely they met, de Tocqueville was writing during the time of the Danish philosopher Søren Kierkegaard. As if he, too, could see the future, Kierkegaard was plagued with anxiety. However, Kierkegaard didn't call anxiety a plague: As he pointed out, anxiety is fundamental to our sense of humanity. Although I'm tempted to discard Kierkegaard's every thought based simply on his ludicrous leap of faith, I can't convince myself to disagree with him about anxiety. His writings about anxiety resonate with me as strongly as anything I've read by Lao Tzu, Schopenhauer, or Leopold.

It's small wonder I've slept so poorly since August of 1979, when I reached a vague, subconscious understanding of the dire straits in which humanity is immersed. More than three decades after that summer of my nineteenth year, "my distress is enormous, boundless," and growing by the day. I envy those who know about ongoing climate change and yet can remain comfortable with that knowledge. If you're among them, perhaps this essay will drag you with me, into the abyss of despair. If so, I encourage you to embrace the prescient words of Edward Abbey: "Action is the antidote to despair."

How bad is our current situation? Desperation is leading to long-shot technical "fixes" on the climate-change front. Naturally, these do not include changing the behavior of people in the industrialized world. As usual, Americans, still affluent relative to people in other nations, can't be bothered because they're too concerned about the industrial economy to worry about persistence of *Homo sapiens*. The occasional thoughtful American writes a letter of apology to his grandchildren, preferring the ease of an apology over the difficulty of action. But most Americans follow the lead of their president, thereby continuing to ignore the issue. Apparently money is more valuable than life on Earth.

CLIMATE CHAOS IS POISED TO KILL US ALL

American actress Lily Tomlin is credited with the expression, "No matter how cynical you become, it's never enough to keep up." With respect to climate science, my own efforts to stay abreast are blown away every week by new data, models, and assessments. It seems no matter how dire the situation becomes, it only gets worse when I check the latest reports.

The response of politicians, heads of non-governmental organizations, and corporate leaders remains the same. They're mired in the dank Swamp of Nothingness. These are the people who know about, and presumably could do something about, our ongoing race to disaster (if only to sound the alarm). Tomlin's line is never more germane than when thinking about their pursuit of a buck at the expense of life on Earth.

Worse than the aforementioned trolls are the media. Fully captured by corporations and the corporate states, the media continue to dance around the issue of climate change. Occasionally a forthright piece is published, but it generally points in the wrong direction, such as suggesting climate scientists and activists be killed (as occurred, for example, in James Delingpole's 7 April 2013 hate-filled article in the *Telegraph*). Most media reports, however, simply ignore or marginalize the issue of climate change.

Even mainstream scientists minimize the message at every turn. As we've known for years, scientists almost invariably underplay climate impacts. I'm not implying conspiracy. Science selects for conservatism. Academia selects for extreme conservatism. These folks are loathe to risk drawing undue attention to themselves by pointing out there might be a threat to civilization. Never mind the near-term threat to our entire species (they couldn't care less about other species). If the truth is dire, they can find another, not-so-dire version. The concept is supported by an article in the February 2013 issue of *Global Environmental Change* pointing out that climate-change scientists routinely underestimate impacts "by erring on the side of least drama."

If you're too busy to read the evidence presented below, here's the bottom line: On a planet 4 C hotter than baseline, all we can prepare for is human extinction (according to Oliver Tickell's 2008 synthesis in the *Guardian*). Tickell is taking a conservative approach, considering humans have not been present at 3.5 C above baseline (i.e., the beginning of the Industrial Revolution, conveniently pegged at 1850, when oil was distilled into gasoline for the first time). According to the United Nations Environment Programme's December 2010 assessment, which does not include self-reinforcing feedback loops, global average temperature of Earth will increase up to 5 C by 2050. To be fair, this assessment does not consider economic collapse, either.

According to Colin Goldblatt, author of a paper published online in the 28 July 2013 issue of *Nature Geoscience*, "The runaway greenhouse may be much easier to initiate than previously thought." Furthermore, as pointed out in the 1 August 2013 issue of *Science*, in the near term Earth's climate will change orders of magnitude faster than at any time during the last 65 million years.

If you think we'll adapt, think again. The rate of evolution trails the rate of climate change by a factor of 10,000, according to a paper in the August 2013 issue of *Ecology Letters*.

The rate of climate change clearly has gone beyond linear, as indicated by the presence of the myriad self-reinforcing feedback loops described below, and now threatens our species with extinction in the near term. Anthropologist Louise Leakey ponders our near-term demise in her 5 July 2013 assessment at *Huffington Post*. In the face of near-term human extinction, Americans view the threat as distant and irrelevant, as illustrated by a 22 April 2013 article in the *Washington Post* based on poll results that echo the long-held sentiment that elected officials should be focused on the industrial economy, not far-away minor nuisances such as climate change.

This essay brings attention to projections and positive feedbacks through 8 September 2013. I have presented much of this information on speaking tours and my website, *Nature Bats Last* (guymcpherson.com). All information and sources are readily confirmed with a minor attempt at scholarship.

Large-scale assessments
Intergovernmental Panel on Climate Change (late 2007):
    1 C by 2100
Hadley Centre for Meteorological Research (late 2008):
    2 C by 2100

United Nations Environment Programme (mid 2009):
3.5 C by 2100

Hadley Centre for Meteorological Research (October
2009): 4 C by 2060

Global Carbon Project, Copenhagen Diagnosis (November
2009): 6 C, 7 C by 2100

United Nations Environment Programme (December
2010): up to 5 C by 2050

These assessments fail to account for significant self-reinforcing feedback loops (i.e., positive feedbacks, the term that implies the opposite of its meaning). These feedback loops exacerbate climate change, thus accelerating the rate at which change occurs. The recently leaked IPCC's vaunted Fifth Assessment will continue the trend as it, too, ignores important feedbacks. On a positive note, major assessments fail to account for economic collapse. However, due to the feedback loops presented below, I strongly suspect it's too late for economic collapse to extend the run of our species.

Taking a broad view

Astrophysicists have long believed Earth was near the center of the habitable zone for humans. Research published in the 10 March 2013 issue of *Astrophysical Journal* indicates Earth is on the inner edge of the habitable zone, and lies within 1 percent of inhabitability (1.5 million km, or about 3 times the distance from Earth to Earth's moon). A minor change in Earth's atmosphere removes human habitat. Unfortunately, we've invoked major changes.

The northern hemisphere is particularly susceptible to accelerated warming, as explained in the 8 April 2013 issue of *Journal of Climate*. The primary driver is the large land:water ratio in the northern hemisphere relative to its southern counterpart, which reduces the ameliorating impact of the marine environment. Two days after the paper appeared in the *Journal of Climate*, a paper in *Nature* confirmed that summers in the northern hemisphere are hotter than they've been for 600 years. As pointed out by Sherwood and Huber in the 25 May 2012 issue of the *Proceedings of the National Academy of Sciences* and then by climate scientist extraordinaire James Hansen in his 15 April 2013 paper, humans cannot survive a wet-bulb temperature of 35 C (95 F). Wet-bulb temperature is defined as the temperature a parcel of air would have if it were cooled to saturation (i.e., dew point). In other words, the wet-bulb temperature corresponds to the air temperature at a relative humidity of 100 percent. A wet-bulb temperature of 95 F can be achieved at 95 F and 100 percent relative humidity and also, for example, at 100 F and 80 percent relative humidity.

As described by the United Nations Advisory Group on Greenhouse Gases in 1990, "Beyond 1 degree C may elicit rapid, unpredictable and non-linear responses that could lead to extensive ecosystem damage." Earth has warmed about 1 C since the beginning of the industrial revolution, according to sensors based on land (cf. instruments aboard satellites). However, plants in the vicinity of Concord, Massachusetts—where records derived from instruments indicate warming of about 1 C—indicate warming of 2.4 C since the 1840s.

Whether you believe the plants or the instruments is irrelevant at the point. We've clearly triggered the types of positive feedbacks the United Nations warned about in 1990. Yet my colleagues and acquaintances think we can and will work our way out of this horrific mess by applying, by itself, the principles of permaculture (which is not to denigrate permaculture, the principles of which are implemented at the mud hut). Reforestation doesn't come close to overcoming combustion of fossil fuels, as pointed out in the 30 May 2013 issue of *Nature Climate Change*. Adding egregious insult to spurting wound, the latest public-education initiative in the United States—the Next Generation Science Standards—buries the relationship between combustion of fossil fuels and planetary warming. The misadventures of the corporate government continue.

Let's ignore the models for a moment and consider only the results of a single briefing to the United Nations Conference of the Parties in Copenhagen (COP15) in 2009. The briefing was prepared by Jamaica's T. Goreau to the Association of Small Island States and titled, "What is the right target for CO2?: 350 ppm is a death sentence for coral reefs and low lying islands, the safe level of CO2 for SIDS is around 260 parts per million." Followers of climate science will recall COP15 as the climate-change meetings thrown under the bus by the Obama administration. A summary of that long-forgotten briefing begins with this statement: "THE LONG-TERM SEA LEVEL THAT CORRESPONDS TO CURRENT CO2 CONCENTRATION IS ABOUT 23 METERS ABOVE TODAY'S LEVELS, AND THE TEMPERATURES WILL BE 6 DEGREES C OR MORE HIGHER. THESE ESTIMATES ARE BASED ON REAL LONG TERM CLIMATE RECORDS, NOT ON MODELS."

In other words, Obama and others in his administration knew near-term extinction of humans was already guaranteed. Even before the dire feedbacks were reported by the scientific community, the Obama administration abandoned climate change as a significant issue because it knew we were done as early as 2009. Rather than shoulder the unenviable task of truth-teller, Obama did as his imperial higher-ups demanded: He lied about collapse, and he lied about climate change. And he still does. Ah, those were the good ol' days, back when atmospheric carbon dioxide concentrations were below 400 parts per million (ppm). We recently blew through the 400 ppm mark for the first time in 3.2 to 5 million years, and 280 ppm is where we began the experiment with industrial civilization. As reported in the journal *Global and Planetary Change* in April 2013, every molecule of atmospheric carbon dioxide since 1980 comes from human emissions. Not to be outdone, methane levels reached an average mean of 1800 parts per billion (ppb) on the morning of 16 June 2013, and seeps are appearing in numerous locations off the eastern coast of the United States. This figure is 1100 ppb higher than pre-industrial peak levels, a figure easily verified by any number of sources. Methane release tracks closely with temperature rise throughout Earth history, including a temperature rise up to about 1 C per year over a decade, according to data from ice cores. Molecule for molecule, methane is twenty times more powerful a greenhouse gas than carbon dioxide in the long term. In the span of a couple decades, methane is up to one hundred times more powerful than carbon dioxide.

Positive feedbacks
Methane hydrates are bubbling out the Arctic Ocean (*Science*, March 2010). According to NASA's CARVE project, these plumes were up to 150 kilometers across as of mid-July 2013. On 9 February 2012 Malcolm Light

forecast extinction of *all life on Earth* by the middle of this century based on methane release from the Arctic Ocean. The analysis predicted extinction of all life in the northern hemisphere in 2031 plus or minus 13 years. Light's analysis, which appeared on the Arctic Methane Emergency Group's website (arctic-news.blogspot.com), seemed premature a few months after he conducted the analysis because it was based on exponential methane release during summer 2011. The data foretelling exponential methane release were subsequently revised and smoothed by U.S. government agencies, with a handful of data points deleted from the dataset. However, subsequent information—most notably from NASA's CARVE project—indicates the grave potential for catastrophic release of methane. Recent trends make Malcolm Light's initial forecast of exponential methane release and subsequent large-scale extinction seem quite prescient, particularly when subsequent analyses are considered. Nafeez Ahmed's thorough analysis in the 5 August 2013 issue of the *Guardian* supports the notion of catastrophically rapid release of methane in the Arctic, as does as Natalia Shakhova's 29 July 2013 YouTube interview with Nick Breeze.

Warm Atlantic water is defrosting the Arctic as it shoots through the Fram Strait (*Science*, January 2011). This breakdown of the thermohaline conveyor belt is happening in the Antarctic as well.

Siberian methane vents have increased in size from less than a meter across in the summer of 2010 to about a kilometer across in 2011 (*Tellus*, February 2011). The media have since ignored the issue, and I know of no results from 2012 or later.

Drought in the Amazon triggered the release of more carbon than the United States in 2010 (*Science*, February 2011). I know of no subsequent observations. Peat in the world's boreal forests is decomposing at an astonishing rate (*Nature Communications*, November 2011), thus releasing carbon into the atmosphere at an accelerating rate.

Invasion of tall shrubs warms the soil by carrying heat into the root zone, hence destabilizing the permafrost (*Environmental Research Letters*, March 2012).

Greenland ice is darkening, thus enhancing absorption of solar radiation (*The Cryosphere*, June 2012).

Methane is being released from the Antarctic, too (*Nature*, August 2012).

Russian forest and bog fires are growing (NASA, August 2012), a phenomenon consequently apparent throughout the northern hemisphere (*Nature Communications*, July 2013). The *New York Times* reports hotter, drier conditions leading to huge fires in western North America as the "new normal" in their 1 July 2013 issue. A paper in the 22 July 2013 issue of the *Proceedings of the National Academy of Sciences* indicates boreal forests are burning at a rate exceeding that of the last 10,000 years.

Cracking of glaciers accelerates in the presence of increased carbon dioxide (*Journal of Physics D: Applied Physics*, October 2012).

The Beaufort Gyre apparently has reversed course (U.S. National Snow and Ice Data Center, October 2012). If subsequent data support the reversal of the Beaufort Gyre from clockwise to counter-clockwise, they indicate that the Gyre will be pulling warm Atlantic water into the Arctic even faster than without the Gyre's reversal.

Exposure to sunlight increases bacterial conversion of exposed soil carbon, thus accelerating thawing of the permafrost (*Proceedings of the National Academy of Sciences*, February 2013).

The microbes have joined the decomposition party, too, according to a paper in the 23 February 2013 issue of *New Scientist.*

Summer ice melt in Antarctica is at its highest level in a thousand years: Summer ice in the Antarctic is melting 10 times quicker than it was 600 years ago, with the most rapid melt occurring in the last 50 years (*Nature Geoscience*, April 2013). Although scientists have long expressed concern about the instability of the West Atlantic Ice Sheet (WAIS), a research paper published in the 28 August 2013 of *Nature* indicates the East Atlantic Ice Sheet (EAIS) has undergone rapid changes in the past five decades. The latter is the world's largest ice sheet and was previously thought to be at little risk from climate change. But it has undergone rapid changes in the past five decades, signaling a potential threat to global sea levels. The EAIS holds enough water to raise sea levels more than 50 meters.

Floods in Canada are sending pulses of silty water out through the Mackenzie Delta and into the Beaufort Sea, thus painting brown a wide section of the Arctic Ocean near the Mackenzie Delta brown (NASA, June 2013). Subsequently darkened Arctic waters absorb more heat from the sun.

Surface meltwater draining through cracks in an ice sheet can warm the sheet from the inside, softening the ice and letting it flow faster, according to a study accepted for publication in the Journal of Geophysical Research: Earth Surface (July 2013). It appears a Heinrich Event has been triggered in Greenland. Consider the description of such an event as provided by Robert Scribbler on 8 August 2013:

In a Heinrich Event, the melt forces eventually reach a tipping point. The warmer water has greatly softened the ice sheet. Floods of water flow out beneath the ice. Ice ponds grow into great lakes that may spill out both over top of the ice and underneath it. Large ice damns (sic) may or may not start to form. All through this time ice motion and melt is accelerating. Finally, a major tipping point is reached and in a single large event or ongoing series of such events, a massive surge of water and ice flush outward as the ice sheet enters an entirely chaotic state. Tsunamis of melt water rush out bearing their vast floatillas (sic) of ice burgs (sic), greatly contributing to sea level rise. And that's when the weather really starts to get nasty. In the case of Greenland, the firing line for such events is the entire North Atlantic and, ultimately the Northern Hemisphere.

Breakdown of the thermohaline conveyor belt is happening in the Antarctic as well as the Arctic, thus leading to melting of Antarctic permafrost (*Scientific Reports*, July 2013).

Loss of Arctic sea ice is reducing the temperature gradient between the poles and the equator, thus causing the jet stream to slow and meander. One result is the creation of weather blocks such as the recent very high temperatures in Alaska. As a result, boreal peat dries and catches fire like a coal seam. The resulting soot enters the atmosphere to fall again, coating the ice surface elsewhere, thus reducing albedo and hastening the melting of ice. Each of these individual phenomena has been reported, albeit rarely, but to my knowledge the dots have not been connected beyond this book. The inability or unwillingness of the media to connect two dots is not surprising, and has been routinely reported. (Dots first connected at *Nature Bats Last*, July 2013.)

Arctic ice is growing darker, hence less reflective (*Nature Climate Change*, August 2013).

Extreme weather events drive climate change, as reported in the 15 August 2013 issue of *Nature* (*Nature*, August 2013).

Ocean acidification, which is occurring at the fastest rate in at least 250 million years, leads to release of less dimethyl sulphide (DMS) by plankton. DMS shields Earth from radiation. (*Nature Climate Change*, online 25 August 2013).

Sea-level rise causes slope collapse, tsunamis, and release of methane, as reported in the September 2013 issue of *Geology*.

Rising ocean temperatures will upset natural cycles of carbon dioxide, nitrogen and phosphorus, hence reducing phytoplankton, the small organisms at the base of the marine food web that sequester atmospheric carbon dioxide and produce oxygen (*Nature Climate Change*, September 2013).

Arctic drilling was fast-tracked by the Obama administration during the summer of 2012.

If I'm doing the math correctly, a single self-reinforcing feedback loop was reported by the scientific community in 2010. The following year brought 4 more, 2012 saw 7 (including the only reversible feedback on the list, the final item), and 2013 has revealed 12 through early September. We're seeing geologic events play out in real time, and they are accelerating. Most of these feedbacks are obvious, based on common sense alone. As I've often pointed out, science merely represents elucidation of the obvious.

Unfortunately, these feedbacks are not additive, they are multiplicative. As nearly as I can distinguish, only the latter feedback process is reversible at a temporal scale relevant to our species. Once the tab on the can of beer is pulled off, there's no keeping the carbon dioxide from bubbling up and out. Regarding the reversibility of the latter feedback, now that we've entered the era of expensive oil I can't imagine we'll voluntarily terminate the process of drilling for oil and gas in the Arctic (or anywhere else).

See how far we've come

Never mind that American naturalist George Perkins Marsh, in a lecture to the Agricultural Society of Rutland County, Vermont, predicted anthropogenic climate change as a result of burning fossil fuels in 1847. Never mind that climate risks have been underestimated for the last 20 Years, or that the IPCC's efforts have failed miserably. After all, climate scientist and professor Kevin Anderson, Deputy Director of the Tyndall Centre in Britain, while speaking to the Cabot Institute in Bristol, U.K. on 6 November 2012 revealed what I've known for years: Politicians and the scientists writing official reports on climate change are lying, and we have less time than most people can imagine. Never mind David Wasdell pointed out at the Tällberg Forum in 2008 that we must have a period of negative radiative forcing merely to end up with a stable, non-catastrophic climate system. Never mind that even the *Atlantic* from 24 November 2012 displayed "five charts about climate change that should have you very, very worried." Never mind that atmospheric carbon dioxide is affecting satellites, as reported by the *Huffington Post* on 11 November 2012. Never mind that even the occasional economic analyst has been telling climate scientists to be persuasive, be brave, and be arrested. Never mind that Peruvian ice requiring 1,600 years to accumulate has melted in the last 25 years, according to a paper in the 4 April 2013 issue of *Science*. And never mind that warming in the interior of large continents in the northern hemisphere has outstripped model predictions in racing to 6-7 C already, according to a paper that tallied temperature rise in China's interior in the 15 May 2013 issue of the *Proceedings of the National Academy of Sciences*.

Never mind all that: Future temperatures likely will be at the higher end of the projected range because the forecasts are all too conservative and also because climate negotiations won't avert catastrophe. The latter tidbit comes from analysis rooted in game theory and was reported in the 23 October 2013 issue of *Proceedings of the National Academy of Sciences*.

Through late March 2013, global oceans have risen approximately ten millimeters per year during the last two years. This rate of rise is over three times the rate of sea level rise during the time of satellite-based observations from 1993 to the present. Ocean temperatures are rising, and have been impacting global fisheries for four decades, according to the 16 May 2013 issue of *Nature*.

Actually, catastrophe is already here, although it's not widely distributed in the United States. Well, not yet, even though the continental U.S. experienced its highest temperature ever in 2012, shattering the 1998 record by a full degree Fahrenheit. The east coast of North America experienced its hottest water temperatures all the way to the bottom of the ocean. The epic dust bowl of 2012 grew and grew and grew all summer long. As pointed out in the March 2004 issue of *Geophysical Research Letters*, disappearing sea ice is expectedly contributing to the drying of the western United States (more definitive research on the topic appeared in the December 2005 issue of *Earth Interactions*). Equally expectedly for those paying attention, the drought arrived 40 years early.

Even conservative climate scientists James Hansen and Makiko Sato are asking whether the loss of ice on Greenland has gone exponential. They are ridiculously calling for a carbon tax to "fix" the "problem." The tentative answer to their question is not promising, based on recent data, including a nearly five-fold increase in melting of Greenland's ice since the 1990s and a stunning melting of 98 percent of Greenland's ice surface between 8 and 15 July 2012.

On a particularly dire note for humanity, climate change causes early death of 400,000 people each year. For example, warming in the Arctic is causing the release of toxic chemicals long trapped in the region's snow, ice, ocean and soil, according to research published in the 24 July 2011 issue of *Nature Climate Change*.

Greenhouse-gas emissions keep rising, and keep setting records. According to 10 June 2013 report by the ever-conservative International Energy Agency (IEA), the horrific trend continued in 2012, when carbon dioxide emissions set a record for the fifth consecutive year. The trend puts disaster squarely in the cross-hairs, with the IEA claiming we're headed for a global-average temperature exceeding 5 C above baseline.

Completely contrary to the popular contrarian myth, global warming has accelerated, with more overall global warming in the past 15 years than the prior 15 years. This warming has resulted about 90 percent of overall global warming going into heating the oceans, and the oceans have been warming dramatically, according to a paper published in the March 2013 issue of *Geophysical Research Letters*. About 30 percent of the ocean warming over the past decade has occurred in the deeper oceans below 700 meters, which is unprecedented over at least the past half century. The death spiral of Arctic sea ice is well under way.

Also in the category of myth-busting comes a study published in the August 2013 issue of the *Proceedings of the National Academy of Sciences*. Changes in solar radiation have no recent impact on global temperature changes. The study found that the amount of solar radiation passing through Earth's atmosphere and reaching the ground globally peaked in the 1930s, substantially decreased from the 1940s to the 1970s, and changed little after that.

Global loss of sea ice matches the trend in the Arctic. It's down, down, and down some more, with the five lowest values on record all happening in the last seven years (through 2012). As reported in a June 2013 issue of *Science*, the Antarctic's ice shelves are melting from below. When interviewed for the associated article in the 13 June

2013 issue of National Geographic, scientists expressed surprise at the rate of change. Color me shocked.

Then see where we're going

The climate situation is much worse than I've led you to believe, and is accelerating far more rapidly than accounted for by models. Even the U.S. Centers for Disease Control and Prevention acknowledges, in a press release dated 6 June 2013, potentially lethal heat waves on the near horizon.

Ice sheet loss continues to increase at both poles, and warming of the West Antarctic Ice Sheet is twice the earlier scientific estimate. Arctic ice is at an all-time low, half that of 1980, and the Arctic lost enough sea ice to cover Canada and Alaska in 2012 alone. In short, summer ice in the Arctic is nearly gone. Furthermore, the Arctic could well be free of ice by summer 2015, an event that last occurred some three million years ago, before the genus *Homo* walked the planet. Among the consequences of declining Arctic ice is extremes in cold weather in northern continents (thus illustrating why "climate change" is a better term than "global warming").

Even the conservative International Energy Agency (IEA) has thrown in the towel, concluding that "renewable" energy is not keeping up with the old, dirty standard sources. As a result, the IEA report dated 17 April 2013 indicates the development of low-carbon energy is progressing too slowly to limit global warming.

The Arctic isn't Vegas—what happens in the Arctic doesn't stay in the Arctic—it's the planet's air conditioner. In fact, as pointed out 10 June 2013 by research scientist Charles Miller of NASA's Jet Propulsion Laboratory: "Climate change is already happening in the Arctic, faster than its ecosystems can adapt. Looking at the Arctic is like looking at the canary in the coal mine for the entire Earth system." On the topic of rapidity of change, a paper in the August 2013 issue of *Ecology Letters* points out that rates of projected climate change dramatically exceed past rates of climatic niche evolution among vertebrate species. In other words, vertebrates cannot evolve or adapt rapidly enough to keep up with ongoing and projected changes in climate.

How critical is Arctic ice? Whereas nearly 80 calories are required to melt a gram of ice at 0 C, adding 80 calories to the same gram of water at 0 C increases its temperature to 80 C. Anthropogenic greenhouse-gas emissions add more than 2.5 trillion calories to Earth's surface every hour (ca. 3 watts per square meter, continuously).

Ocean acidification associated with increased atmospheric carbon dioxide is proceeding at an unprecedented rate and could trigger mass extinction by itself. Already, half the Great Barrier Reef has died during the last three decades. And ocean acidification is hardly the only threat on the climate-change front. As one little-discussed example, atmospheric oxygen levels are dropping to levels considered dangerous for humans, particularly in cities.

An increasing number of scientists agree that warming of 4 to 6 C causes a dead planet. And, they go on to say, we'll be there by 2060. Earth-system scientist Clive Hamilton concludes in his April 2013 book *Earthmasters* that "without [atmospheric sulphates associated with industrial activity]...Earth would be an extra 1.1 C warmer." In other words, collapse takes us directly to 2 C above baseline within a matter of weeks. Several other academic scientists have concluded, in the refereed journal literature no less, that the 2 C mark is essentially impossible (for example, see the review paper by Mark New and colleagues published in the 29 November 2010 issue of the *Philosophical Transactions of the Royal Society A*). The German Institute for International and Security Affairs concluded 2 June 2013 that a 2 C rise in global-average temperature is no longer feasible (and *Spiegel* agrees, finally, in their 7 June 2013 issue), while the ultra-conservative International Energy Agency concludes that, "coal will nearly overtake oil as the dominant energy source by 2017...without a major shift away from coal, average global temperatures could rise by 6 degrees Celsius by 2050, leading to devastating climate change." In an October 2012 interview, climate scientist Paul Beckwith indicated Earth could warm by 6 C within a decade. If you think his view is extreme, consider the reconstruction of regional and global temperature for the past 11,300 years published in *Science* in March 2013. It indicates an extremely rapid increase in global-average temperature is under way, with no end in sight.

It's not merely scientists who know where we're going. The Pentagon is bracing for public dissent over climate and energy shocks, as reported by Nafeez Ahmed in the 14 June 2013 issue of the *Guardian*. According to Ahmed's article: "Top secret US National Security Agency (NSA) documents disclosed by the *Guardian* have shocked the world with revelations of a comprehensive US-based surveillance system with direct access to Facebook, Apple, Google, Microsoft and other tech giants. New Zealand court records suggest that data harvested by the NSA's Prism system has been fed into the Five Eyes intelligence alliance whose members also include the UK, Canada, Australia and New Zealand." In short, the "Pentagon knows that environmental, economic and other crises could provoke widespread public anger toward government and corporations" and is planning accordingly. Such "activity is linked to the last decade of US defence planning, which has been increasingly concerned by the risk of civil unrest at home triggered by catastrophic events linked to climate change, energy shocks or economic crisis—or all three." The global police state has arrived, and just in time to keep the blinders firmly on the majority of "first-world" humans.

THE ABSURDITY OF AUTHENTICITY

I'm often accused—or credited, depending on one's perspective—of leading an authentic life. As nearly as I can tell, the accusation or accolade refers to the following definition from Merriam and Webster: true to one's own personality, spirit, or character.

Fundamentally, aren't we all true to our personality, spirit, and character? How could we act otherwise, in the absence of multiple personalities? I have concluded that we've been captured by the culture in which we're immersed. We are unable to escape without killing ourselves, yet the culture is killing us.

We're six millennia into the culture of Abrahamic religions. We're more than two millennia into western civilization and the six questions of Socrates: (1) What is good? (2) What is piety? (3) What is virtue? (4) What is courage? (5) What is moderation? (6) What is justice? Furthermore, every person reading these words is a product of an industrial civilization that depends upon expansive use of fossil fuels.

Is this the only way to live? Is this the best way to live? Do our hyper-connected, high-tech lives lead us along paths of excellence, in the spirit of Socrates?

This culture is steeped in patriarchy and depends upon violence for its continuation. Is it safe to assume this culture is the ultimate expression of our humanity? Is it safe to assume that this culture is the best we can do simply because this culture is the only one we have known? Is it safe to assume there is no other way beyond the hierarchical omnicide we've come to depend upon for money, water, food, and personal identity?

Questioning this culture and its underlying assumptions follows the model promoted and popularized by Socrates. Answering these questions requires one to step outside the normalcy bias and profound enculturation of the way we live. Asking challenging questions, much less answering them, requires enormous courage when the questions themselves refuse to validate, much less approve, this irredeemably corrupt system.

I do not claim to know the answers to these questions. I'm not certain they have answers independent of the person pondering them and his or her personal experiences. I nonetheless believe it is important to ask the questions and develop personal responses to them. As a result, I will tackle these and related questions in this chapter. For the most part, culture discourages us from asking, much less answering, most of these questions.

Questions, questions, and more questions

Throughout our lives, we spend considerable time seeking feedback from people and institutions, but the feedback we seek generally falls within a small subset of important issues. Furthermore, I question the wisdom of seeking validation, much less approval, within the realm of an irredeemably corrupt system.

Some of us seek to conduct meaningful lives. However, the universe imposes upon us a meaningless existence. There is no meaning beyond the meaning(s) we create. In attempting to create meaning, which often involves attempts to outrun our mortality, we generate distractions. We occasionally call them objectives, goals, or acts of service to others. And the result is our legacy.

Yet it's too late to leave a better world for future generations of humans. The concept of leaving a legacy becomes moot when staring into the abyss of near-term human extinction. What, then, is the point? Are we, in the words of English poet Frances Cornford, "magnificently unprepared for the long littleness of life"?

As we seek feedback about the conduct of our lives, we simultaneously seek distractions. The distractions include the movies we watch, the books we read, the trips we take, the discussions in which we engage. The line blurs between distractions and authentic work until we are defined by the combination. The totality becomes who we are. The nature of our distractions is what makes us human, in the sense of differentiating us from other primates. Non-human primates don't read books, much less discuss them. Such distractions do not enable our survival and in that sense are not "necessities" (cf. food, water, shelter). However, they are not necessarily "luxuries," either. Apparently there are shades of existential gray.

Shades of gray

Shades of existential gray are evident in our pursuit of meaningful lives. How do we differentiate between necessity and luxury? How do we distinguish what we want from what we need? And are these distinctions important?

When I began the ongoing process of walking away from the omnicide of industrial civilization, I felt I had no choice. My inner voice overrode outer culture. I have subsequently come to realize that most people born into this set of living arrangements are literally and figuratively incapable of making a similar choice. Distinguishing between needs and wants, between necessity and luxury, is hardly clear.

Occasionally we turn to wise elders in our attempts infuse our lives with meaning. Kurt Vonnegut often wrote, in response to the question about meaning, that we're here to fart around. His son Mark, between the loony bin and Harvard Medical School, responded to the question, "Why are we here?" with the following comment: "We are here to help each other through this, whatever this is."

I love Mark Vonnegut's response, but it fails to acknowledge that service to others is important *and* it's a trap. Service to others is no longer virtuous when the entrapment includes self-inflicted harm (including emotional or psychological suffering).

As the Buddha pointed out more than two millennia ago, life is suffering. Do we have an obligation to minimize suffering? Does that obligation extend to our individual selves, as well as to other humans? Does it extend to non-human species?

German philosopher Arthur Schopenhauer famously defined happiness as the alleviation of suffering, implying a temporary condition. The pursuit of happiness—from Schopenhauer's perspective, the alleviation of suffering—is a right guaranteed by the founding document of the United States, but I've no idea why it's guaranteed or if it stops at the alleviation of suffering. If the alleviation of suffering qualifies as happiness, then it seems wearing shoes that are two sizes too small is a great strategy for producing happiness, if only at the end of the day when the shoes are removed from one's feet.

If happiness goes beyond the alleviation of suffering, perhaps it includes joy. But the notion of such an idea drags into the discussion the notion of documentation, hence measurement. How do we measure joy? Is it the same as the bliss produced by ignorance? How do we know when we've stumbled upon it? And if joy is meritorious, even at the expense of suffering by another, how do we balance the existential books?

Consider, for example, a single example for the Abrahamic religions (aka patriarchy): marriage. Do we have an obligation to minimize the pain when a monogamous relationship become personally painful, or even a matter of indifference (i.e., lacking daily joy)? Contemporary culture suggests we muddle through, in sickness and health, until death. And then, the ultimate personal endpoint solves the problem of suffering.

The cost of happiness

If happiness is a goal, and if that happiness extends beyond the mere alleviation of suffering, how do we evaluate happiness? If our own happiness comes at the expense of another, how do we justify our gain? Equally importantly, but rarely considered, is the converse question: If our suffering brings happiness to another, how do we justify the personal pain? Is our own suffering less important than that of another?

How do we minimize suffering? Is such a quest restricted to humans, or are other organisms included? What is the temporal frame of the quest? Does it extend beyond the moment, perhaps to months or years? Does it extend beyond the personal to include other individuals?

We could minimize suffering to humans and other animals by playing solitaire in the woods. But even that seemingly humble act takes life. Tacking on the seemingly simple acquisition of water, food, clothing, and shelter for a single human being in the industrialized world brings horrific suffering to humans and other animals. Attending to the needs of the 7.1 billion humans currently inhabiting Earth comes at tremendous cost to the water, soils, and non-human species on the planet. Contemplating the *desires* of an increasing number of people on an overpopulated globe is enough to drive a thinking person to despair.

There is nothing inherently wrong with pleasure, yet the Greek word for "pleasure" forms the root of the English word "hedonism." According to my pals Merriam and Webster, hedonism propounds that pleasure or happiness is the sole or chief good in life. When stated in this manner, pleasure seems to have taken a step too far. But drawing the line between personal pleasure and hedonism is no mean feat. Less often considered is the line we draw between personal suffering and the attendant happiness of others.

But, lest we take that step too far, we should remember that the idea of hedonism some 2,500 years ago when Socrates was haunting the Mediterranean region was a bit different than the idea today. Back then, humans comprised a tiny drop in the large bucket known as Earth. The quest for personal pleasure and happiness at that time would have essentially zero impact on the natural world relative to the impact of today's quest for gratification by 7.1 billion people on an this ever-shrinking and -depleted orb.

When my happiness requires the suffering of another, is my happiness warranted? When the pleasure of another requires my suffering, is the suffering warranted? Does failing to contemplate questions about our needs and desires commit us to nihilism? Does living within the Age of Industry, hence participating in untold horrors to humans and other organisms, violate the Socratic notion of good?

What about empire?
American Empire is merely the most lethal manifestation of industrial civilization, hence any civilization. Because this

culture is inextricably interconnected with this civilization, I have concluded that contemporary culture is worthy of our individual and collective condemnation. Walking away from empire is necessary but insufficient to terminate this horrific culture.

As nearly as I can determine, maintaining American Empire—or any empire, for that matter—requires three fundamental elements: obedience at home, oppression abroad, and destruction of the living planet. Unpacking these three attributes seems a worthy exercise, even acknowledging Voltaire's observation: "It is dangerous to be right in matters on which the established authorities are wrong."

Obedience at home means capitulating to culture and the government. It means abandoning a culture of resistance in favor of the nanny state. It means allowing the government to control the people instead of the other way around. It means giving up responsibility for oneself and one's neighbors and expecting the government to deal with all issues. Considering the excellent record of the government in transferring wealth from the poor to the rich while promoting an economy rooted in war, I've no idea why the people with whom I interact are fans of this government.

Oppression abroad is obvious to anybody paying attention to American foreign policy during the last hundred years. The government of the United States of Absurdity extracts taxes from the citizenry to build the most lethal killing force in the history of the world. This military, supported by cultural messages and therefore most of the consumer-oriented citizenry, is then used to extract materials such as fossil fuels from other countries. The resulting "riches" enjoyed by Americans serve to pacify the masses, embolden the government, and enrich the corporations that exert strong influence over both the media and the government.

Destruction of the living planet is imperative if we are to support seven billion people on the planet, many of whom want "their" baubles. Are we not entitled to transport ourselves around the world, dine at fancy restaurants for a few hours' work at minimum wage, entertain ourselves with music and movies, and all the rest on an essentially limitless list? Where do the materials originate for each of these endeavors? Are we so filled with hubris that we believe driving dozens of species to extinction every day is our right? Do we lack the humility—and even the conscience—to treat non-human species with respect?

Each of these three broad elements serves a subset of humans at the expense of others. Although obedience to culture prevents us from being viewed as "odd" to our straitjacketed acquaintances, it also serves the oppressors. Giving up on radicalism—i.e., getting to the root—fails to serve our needs while lessening our humanity. But it nicely serves those who pull the levers of industry.

Perhaps it is time we heed the words of deceased American social critic Christopher Hitchens: "To be in opposition is not to be a nihilist. And there is no decent or charted way of making a living at it. It is something you are, and not something you do."

Imperialism has consequences

The U.S. Constitution and Bill of Rights are bobbing along the same waves as social justice and environmental protection, sold down the river by a nation addicted to growth for the sake of growth (the ideology of a cancer cell). Indeed, it seems very little matters to the typical American beyond economic growth. And for that, most importantly, we need an uninterrupted supply of crude oil. We need the Carter Doctrine—the world's oil belongs to us—and an unhealthy dose of faux patriotism.

Our lives are imbued with faux patriotism. We are manipulated by the war-loving corporate media and the war-loving politicians that, unsurprisingly, are enriched by war. We support the troops that bring us the baubles we're convinced we deserve, and we rarely question the real, underlying costs of the baubles.

Support the troops. It's the rallying cry of an entire nation. It's the slogan pasted on many of the bumpers in the United States.

Supporting the troops is pledging your support for the empire. Supporting the troops supports the occupation of sovereign nations because might makes right. Supporting the troops supports wanton murder of women and children throughout the world. And men, too. Supporting the troops supports obedience at home and oppression abroad. Supporting the troops throws away every ideal on which this country allegedly is founded. Supporting the troops supports the ongoing destruction of the living planet in the name of economic growth. Supporting the troops therefore hastens our extinction in exchange for a few dollars. Supporting the troops means caving in to Woodrow Wilson's neo-liberal agenda, albeit cloaked as contemporary neo-conservatism (cf. hope and change). Supporting the troops trumpets power as freedom and fascism as democracy.

I'm not suggesting the young people recruited into the military are at fault. Victims of civilization and a lifetime of cultural programming—like me, and perhaps you—they're looking for job security during a period of economic contraction. The entire process is working great for the oppressors pulling the levers of industry.

Perhaps most importantly, supporting the troops means giving up on resistance. Resistance is all we have, and all we've ever had. We say we're mad as hell and we claim we're not going to take it anymore. But, sadly, we gave up on resistance of any kind years ago.

We act as if America's cultural revolution never happened. We act as if we never questioned the dominant paradigm in an empire run amok, as if we never experienced Woodstock and the Summer of Love, bra-burning hippies and war-torn teenagers, Rosa Parks and the Cuyahoga River. We're right back in the 1950s, swimming in culture's main stream instead of questioning, resisting, and protesting.

We've moved from the unquestioning automatons of Aldous Huxley and George Orwell to the firebrands of a radical counter-cultural worldview and back again. A generational sea change swept us from post-war "liberators" drunk on early 1950s propaganda to revolutionaries willing to take risks in defense of late 1960s ideals. The revolution gained steam through the 1970s, but lost its way when the U.S. industrial economy hit the speed bump of domestic peak oil. The Carter Doctrine coupled with Ronald Reagan's soothing pack of lies was the perfect match to our middle-aged comfort, so we abandoned the noble ideals of earlier days for another dose of palliative propaganda. Three decades later, we've swallowed so much Soma we couldn't find a hint of revolution in Karl Marx's *Communist Manifesto*.

In short, the pillars of social justice and environmental protection rose from the cesspool of ignorance to become shining lights for an entire generation. And then we let them fall back into the swamp. The very notion that *others* matter—much less that those others are worth fighting for—has been relegated to the dustbin of history.

A line from Eugene Debs, five-time candidate of the Socialist party for U.S. president, comes to mind: "While there is a lower class I am in it, while there is a criminal element I am of it; while there is a soul in prison, I am not free."

I don't harbor any illusions about my freedom. I live in Police State America.

Imperial illusions

Ultimately, I wonder why any of us bothers trying to be a good person As Ernest Hemingway indicated: "The best people possess a feeling for beauty, the courage to take risks, the discipline to tell the truth, the capacity for sacrifice. Ironically, their virtues make them vulnerable; they are often wounded, sometimes destroyed."

Vulnerability isn't so bad. But few knowingly bring on their own destruction. Instead, I suspect most humans— even those who consider themselves good—actually benefit from and even promote contemporary culture, the problems with which are legion. Do good people promote patriarchy? Do they pursue and promote the notions of marriage and monogamy even when knowing these ideas are steeped in the patriarchy of a culture gone seriously awry? Marriage and monogamy are obligations of empire rather than outcomes of natural law. Instead of abiding and supporting imperialism, shall good people attempt to reduce or eliminate patriarchy, hence civilization, one act at a time?

When we recognize patriarchy and its impacts, where does that leave those of us pursuing authenticity? Indeed, attempting to conduct an authentic life in a culture dominated by patriarchy and engendering destruction is analogous to pursuing meaning in an uncaring universe. Does authenticity have meaning in such a universe? Is authenticity a desirable goal, if goals are merely cogs in the machine of a culture run amok? Is authenticity another stumbling block on the road to happiness? Is authenticity yet another piece of propaganda promoted by the thieves and liars pulling the levers of civilization to trap decent people into lives of service? Do we ultimately and perhaps unwittingly serve civilization, hence omnicide, when attempting to serve humanity?

If a life of service is a trap, why step into the trap? In avoiding the trap are we embracing nihilism, "a viewpoint that traditional values and beliefs are unfounded and that existence is senseless and useless"? And, if so, does the embrace constitute a pact with the proverbial devil?

As individuals and a society, have we become so broken we cannot pursue the truth about ourselves and our culture? Have we become so marginalized, demoralized, and humiliated by this insane culture that we are no longer able to rise up against cultural insanity?

IDENTITY CRISIS

Entering the nation's heartland with my wife and ancient dog in December 2012, I was reminded of a previous trip to America's breadbasket. Thoreau's classic words came to mind as I stood in a kitchen slightly larger than the house I occupy. A sign on the wall read, "Simplify." I nearly recommended, as a decent start, throwing away the nearby sign reading, "Simplify: Throw Everything Out."

En route, we drove across the plains of San Augustin, home of the Very Large Array (VLA). The VLA brings to mind how much time, energy, and fiat currency we spend looking for answers out there. As if our problems and predicaments can be solved if we just look long enough into deep space (hence into deep time). Maybe the aliens will save us, if we behave.

Or maybe not. Perhaps we could have spent all that time, energy, and fiat currency looking inward instead. I suspect the costs would have been lower in every case, and the rewards greater.

We spent the night in Dodge City, Kansas and reached our destination the following day. As such, we were able to get the hell out of Dodge and also proclaim we're not in Kansas anymore, all in the same day. Obviously, the twin proclamations made the trip worthwhile.

Turning my own thoughts inward in the wake of the solstice, I wrote the following ode to the living planet. Channeling Nero, I share it here.

Winter solstice
I thought my darkest day was me, running to you,
forsaking the life I loved.
That hopeful day, so long ago, was challenging,
but not nearly as difficult as this.
The only thing worse than me running way
is this society pushing Nature away.
When I ran away I had hope for the living planet
and I got along fine.
When we push Nature away, we're deep in a well
and we've destroyed all that matters on this lonely planet.
This pain is greater than I could have imagined,
perhaps worse than I can bear.
My heart's been shattered, ripped out,
and is lying in pieces on the indifferent ground.
I don't know what to do and I don't know what I want
but I know I don't want this.
It's not just that I'm in love with the living planet,
although that alone would be profound.
It's that I love her madly, deeply, uncontrollably,
which causes entirely too much pain.
I miss her so, so badly.
I yearn for signs of her wit.
I miss her so, so badly.
I long to gaze into her wild places.
I miss her so, so badly.
I think about her every waking minute.
During the rare moments of fitful sleep

she fills my dreams.
I want to see her and hear her and smell her and feel her
and touch her and taste her.
I want to share what we used to share
and know what we used to know
when we were human animals,
not believing we were gods.
More than she could ever know,
I miss her, as she fades away.
More than she could ever know,
I love her, as she is pummeled to oblivion.
More than she could ever know,
I need her—we need her—as we collectively commit ecocide.
I've long recognized the need to protect what we love.
Either I have little company or we hate Nature.
Maybe both.
The days grow longer now
but not brighter.

Indecision

As attentive readers know by now, I'm a lifelong educator. In fact, the most common insult hurled my way by anonymous online commentators is "lifelong academic."

Ouch. That hurts.

In the hallowed halls, ego is everything. Indeed, it's difficult for me to imagine a profession that selects, to a greater extent than academia, for a huge ego. Shepherding a single refereed journal article through the process of publication builds more callus tissue than swinging a pick and shovel for two years. Multiply by dozens of articles, hundreds of public presentations, and a handful of books, and you can begin to understand why the average academic has an ego slightly larger than hell and half of Asia.

Several years into a new life devoid of regular interaction with inmates and honors students, I'm having the sort of identity crisis described by Dmitry Orlov in his excellent book, *Reinventing Collapse*. According to Orlov, middle-aged men—specifically those aged 45 to 55, nicely bracketing the age I departed the ivory tower (49) and my current age as I write these words (53)—experienced the highest rate of mortality as the Soviet Union collapsed. The two most common causes: suicide and suicide by alcohol. I doubt I'll go either route, but it's easy to understand why Family Providers would experience suicidal depression when their ability to provide for their families slips away like a cat-burglar in the dead of night.

I've come to the point of not respecting myself, which is a dangerous place. In moving to the rock-pile in the desert where the mud hut sits, I failed. I moved to the wrong place at the wrong time with the wrong people.

My identity has been shattered. I lost myself in my quest to build a decent future. Future-motivated my entire life, I have come to realize the heartbreak of such an approach when the future is short and bleak.

I went from being *somebody*—somebody who mattered to many people—to somebody for whom essentially nobody cares. Not my ex-colleagues, not my ex-friends, not my parents, not my siblings.

When somebody—*anybody*—expresses admiration for what I've done, I respond like a puppy getting a treat. I've become that desperate for accolades. When somebody asks me to do something, I do it so he'll like me. I'm a teenager all over again, complete with teenage angst.

I'm mired in an identity crisis. I've attempted to reinvent myself, and it hasn't worked. My passion arises only when I speak in public and when I assume the role as educator at the mud hut. Although I'm increasingly indifferent about this place, I am compelled to share it. I am often criticized for continuing my educational efforts here at Barefoot College. During the last few years, I have hosted hundreds of visitors, showing how we might muddle through an ambiguous future for a few more years if we work together. In return, many people question whether I should be demonstrating this durable set of living arrangements to potential future marauders. Most of the people posing the question are anthropocentric, short-sighted, narcissistic cowards commenting anonymously on forums focused on economic collapse.

I am not surprised many people fail to understand that we're all in this together. Our culture has driven us apart, valuing competition over cooperation. I am not surprised many people fail to understand that, as the expression goes, divided we fall. And so we are. Our culture has promoted faux individualism instead of real collaboration. It's all about me and my stuff, me and my success, me and my ego in this hyper-indulgent morass of American exceptionalism. It's small wonder, then, that many people fail to understand the importance, to me, of educating others. It's everything to me, more important than life itself.

I am profoundly committed to a life of service, a commitment I attribute to my lack of free will. For me, a life lived otherwise is not worth living, even knowing that service is a trap.

I recognize that it's too late to save society, and industrialized society is irredeemable, regardless.

Capitalism is assumed to be the best, most efficient economic system, but I think it's better described as a pathology than an economic system. I recognize, too, that it's too late to save our species beyond a few more years. In light of this knowledge, I'll keep moving seemingly immovable individuals beyond their comfort points. I'll inject empathy, therefore resistance, into a sociopathic culture largely devoid of people willing to stand in opposition to the mainstream. I'll move individuals beyond dark thoughts and into the light of a new world, however brief. I'll move them beyond inaction. I'll move them beyond the oppression of civilization and into the brave new world of a life that gives as well as taking.

Or die trying.

In addition to promoting service, I'm a fan of the gift economy (which is *not* based on barter). Further into words that matter, I differentiate between building social capital and contributing to a decent human community.

My customary gifts include hosting visitors at the mud hut, delivery of presentations for no charge, and copies of my latest book at my cost (or, to those interested in an electronic version of the page proofs, no cost at all). Here at the mud hut, I strive to promote and expand the extant gift economy. This approach makes perfect sense, considering how we began this relationship more than four years ago, when my partners on these 2.7 acres offered my wife and me the gift of an acre (we declined, and we now share the property). In the name of comfort for our friends and neighbors, we barter, too, and sometimes work within the customary system of fiat currency. But I prefer an economy of gifts, which has been the prevailing model for most of our existence as human animals. Gifting removes the pressure associated with placing monetary value on the exchange of goods and services in a barter system. And, to me at least, it seems more compassionate and personal than other alternatives.

Many people believe they are doing themselves a favor by building social capital. I hear this phrase often, and I bristle every time. Employing the root word of a heinous system that developed as the industrial revolution began is hardly a sure-fire strategy for winning friends and (positively) influencing people. The process of "building social capital" equates connivance with decency. Analogous to use of a barter system, the act of building social capital suggests a deposit is being made, and will be drawn upon later, perhaps with interest (i.e., usury).

In contrast to developing social capital, I believe we should work to contribute to a decent human community. As an aside, I'm often asked why I use the phrase, "human community" instead of "community." This is exactly the type of question I have come to expect from individuals who wrongly believe we are the most important species on Earth. We're destroying virtually every aspect of the living planet, and yet we believe we're the foundation on which robust ecosystems depend. Viewing one's place in a human community, and one's contribution to that human community, is analogous to development of a gift economy. By striving to contribute, instead of invest, I can focus on developing life-affirming ties instead of dreaming about the return on my investment. By serving my neighbors, rather than determining how my neighbors can serve me, I become an integral part of a valuable system. As such, the whole, holistic system becomes increasingly durable.

Sharing gifts to develop a durable set of living arrangements within a decent human community: If you can imagine a better goal, please let me know.

Ties that bind

I've hosted hundreds of visitors here, and I've spoken and written often about this rock-pile in the desert as an example of a decent human community. Three threads bring together the few hundred people within five miles of the mud hut.

First and perhaps foremost, the humans here love this place. Consider the examples at either end of the fiat-currency continuum. There are several financially wealthy people here. They could live anywhere, but they choose to live here. The majority of my human neighbors, though, choose to live in dire financial poverty. A mile up the road is a land trust with 13 members who share life on 19 acres. They grow their food and share a common well near the center of the property. They could live in dire financial poverty anywhere, but they choose to live here.

Second, there is a profound respect for self-reliance in this locale. If you can't fix it, learn how. If it's an emergency, learn quickly. The preferred route is to teach yourself. If that doesn't work, you are welcome to call one of the neighbors, most of whom have been pursuing self-reliance for many years. They know about building structures, installing electrical lines, repairing the plumbing, changing the carburetor, growing food, tending animals, mending clothes, and mending fences.

And you'd better not call the expensive plumber in the town 30 miles away. Not when your neighbors need the work and appreciate the companionship and the Federal

Reserve Notes. As John Steinbeck wrote in *Grapes of Wrath*: "If you're in trouble, or hurt, or need—go to the poor people. They're the only ones that'll help—the only ones."

Finally, the appreciation for diversity here is striking. Most of us claim to tolerate other races, creeds, and points of view. But that claim comes up well short, in many of my experiences. And tolerance isn't nearly as much fun as appreciation. Here, we appreciate diversity in its myriad forms. My favorite example is the combination New Year's Eve and house-warming party I crashed a couple years ago. About 20 of us were attending another party. Two of the party-goers had been invited to a party at the home of the financially wealthy couple up the road. So we all went.

We were welcomed, of course. The party was attended by 150 or more people. At one point during the festivities, I happened to notice one of the well-dressed hosts chatting with a cowboy from the cattle company. The cowboy was dressed to the proverbial nines, including the requisite felt hat, pearl-button cowboy shirt, vest, starched blue jeans, and ostrich-skin boots. I suspect you'd be hard pressed to find two people in this country with more disparate political views. They were joined by a man from the land trust. His appearance reflected his living arrangements, with limited access to fiat currency and water. The three men continued an animated, thoughtful conversation for 30 minutes or so, as if they cared about each other. Which they do.

I'm not suggesting it's all rainbows and butterflies here, much less that the years ahead will bring nothing but good times. We have our differences, especially here on this hectare. But these ties that bind keep me here, at least so far.

There are many attributes that could keep us apart. But there are even more that can hold us together, if we allow. I'd like to believe the latter is stronger than the former, despite the tendency of civilized humans to find an "other" in our midst.

Back to identity

The issue of identity (i.e., ego) is far worse in the United States than the situation described by Orlov in the Soviet Union. As becomes apparent during the holidays, when casual conversation is on the menu during every seasonal festivity, our identities are completely bundled with how we earn money. What do you think people mean when they ask, "What do you do?" In every case with which I'm familiar, they are inquiring how I earn money.

Knowing where the entire enterprise of generating cash is headed, I tell people I'm a sharecropper and organic gardener. Oh, and by the way, that right hand of mine, the one you just shook, milked a couple of goats this morning. Then I ask people what they love.

I can suck the air out of room—any room, regardless of size or number of people present—in a matter of seconds.

I'm a sharecropper, organic gardener, and milker of goats, as well as a democrat, a republican, a liberal, a conservative, a radical, an idealist, a pragmatist, a teacher, a mentor, a scientist, a writer, a skeptic, a scholar, a cheese-maker, a son, a brother, a husband, a lover, and a human animal. I'm comfortable with my beliefs and personal philosophy. I've thought deeply about my tiny place in this enormous universe, and I've come to value humility over hubris. And still I'm having an identity crisis. A crisis of confidence. An ego-crushing moment. The longer the industrial economy lasts, the more my identity is pummeled, along with my hope for the living planet. Every day under the rule of Athena drives me further into despair. It's as if my ego were a proxy for the planetary rate of extinction. Considering the effort I've put into defining myself and my place in the universe, I can only imagine the difficulty ahead for the typical American drone. He values his imperial role and fails to recognize the empire for what it is. He gets his news from the television and affiliated media outlets and fails to recognize that form of propaganda for what it is. His sense of entitlement is exceeded only by his ignorance of the role nature plays in his survival. And yet, he's ahead of me.

After all, unlike the American drone, I'm clueless about what to do. I've invested heavily in a reasonably sane set of living arrangements, only to have nature call me further down her path. I'm attempting to serve as a witness, and occasionally a warrior, as the living planet tries to survive the insults of industry. I'm trying to show another—hence, contrarian—way, for a world gone mad. And in return, I'm unappreciated as never before in memory (including even my final decade at the university as viewed through the lens of my dean and department head).

I recognize the necessity of total revolution, but I don't yet see it. The wisdom of activist spiritual teacher Vimala Thakar surfaces in my mind: "In a time when the survival of the human race is in question, to continue with the status quo is to cooperate with insanity, to contribute to chaos. When darkness engulfs the spirit of the people, it is urgent for concerned people to awaken, to rise to revolution."

Obviously, Thakar was an optimist. I love her inclusive approach. And although darkness has engulfed the spirit of the people, I fail to see the awakening at a scale relevant to the task at hand. Impatience grows within me.

With the exception of plunging into the wild or continuing to serve as an unappreciated model immersed in agrarian anarchy, my options are limited. I'm too old to die young, and it's very late to start anew. Returning to the civilized life of an educator has limited appeal and prospects that are even more limited, considering the general perspective on my sanity (or lack thereof). And then there's the moral imperative I feel, well expressed by social reformer and statesman Frederick Douglass: "I prefer to be true to myself, even at the hazard of incurring the ridicule of others, rather than to be false, and to incur my own abhorrence."

Where does this lead? In my case, it leads to utter confusion once I get beyond the notion of continuing to teach. As was recently pointed out to me by somebody a little older than me, and a lot a wiser, "in the end it doesn't matter who you're with if you can't unlock the contents of your own skull."

Which takes us right back to me and my self-indulgence. What to do, in the limited time left at my disposal? The temporal limitations come in two forms: (1) I'm too old to die young (and also too poor to start anew) and (2) the industrial era is nearing its end. Without fuel at the filling stations and water coming out the taps, paid positions at small, selective, liberal-arts colleges will be hard to come by (and meaningless). The day is coming far sooner than most people think. With luck, the forthcoming Lehman-on-steroids moment or a rapid dose of hyperinflation will terminate industrial civilization, thus making the decision on my behalf, and soon. If this latter statement reveals my cowardice, then it also indicates the extreme nature of my indecision.

THE THIRD INDUSTRIAL REVOLUTION WILL NOT BE TELEVISED

As author and activist Derrick Jensen points out, this "culture as a whole and most of its members are insane." I continue to be surprised at the number of people who believe in infinite growth on a finite planet. I continue to be amazed at the number of people who believe a politician cares about them, and that their favorite politician will act in their best interests. I continue to be surprised at the number of people who actually believe in the political process. I continue to be amazed at the number of people who support civilization, knowing it is killing us all. I'm even more surprised, though, at the number of people who claim ignorance about the costs and consequences of industrial civilization.

As pointed out by French author and Nobelist in literature André Gide: "Everything that needs to be said has already been said. But since no one was listening, everything must be said again." So, here I go, saying it again.

Apparently I'm a very slow learner. It's a bad, sad time. I hate this culture.

It's worse than all of the above, though. There are a significant number of people who believe we can continue the omnicide, and that doing so is a good idea. Consider, for example, proponents of the Third Industrial Revolution.

The five pillars of the Third Industrial Revolution infrastructure are listed below. After pasting a brief description directly from Wikipedia (in italics), I dismantle each of the pillars.

1. Shifting to Renewable Energy: Renewable forms of energy—solar, wind, hydro, geothermal, ocean waves, and biomass—make up the first of the five pillars of the Third Industrial Revolution. While these energies still account for a small percentage of the global energy mix, they are growing rapidly as governments mandate targets and benchmarks for their widespread introduction into the market and their falling costs make them increasingly competitive.

"Renewable" sources of energy are derivatives of oil. Oil is the master material. The availability and price of oil control every other "resource." The absurdity and hopelessness of switching to extra-oil sources has been the subject of myriad articles and books, so I will not belabor the point.

2. Buildings as Power Plants: New technological breakthroughs make it possible, for the first time, to design and construct buildings that create all of their own energy from locally available renewable energy sources, allowing us to reconceptualize the future of buildings as "power plants". The commercial and economic implications are vast and far reaching for the real estate industry and, for that matter, Europe and the world. In 25 years from now, millions of buildings—homes, offices, shopping malls, industrial and technology parks—will be constructed to serve as both "power plants" and habitats. These buildings will collect and generate energy locally from the sun, wind, garbage, agricultural and forestry waste, ocean waves and tides, hydro and geothermal—enough energy to provide for their own power needs as well as surplus energy that can be shared.

First, see my comment above regarding "renewable" energy sources. They are a well-promoted myth. Second, consider if you will, the reality of our collective situation 25 years from now. If human beings persist on this planet—and that's a significant "if," based on the various paths by which we are vigorously pursuing human extinction—then it's difficult to imagine a scenario that includes an industrial economy at the scale of the globe. We can have an industrial economy or we can have a living planet, but we cannot have both over another few years.

3. Deploying Hydrogen and other storage technologies in every building and throughout the infrastructure to store intermittent energies. To maximize renewable energy and to minimize cost it will be necessary to develop storage methods that facilitate the conversion of intermittent supplies of these energy sources into reliable assets. Batteries, differentiated water pumping, and other media, can provide limited storage capacity. There is, however, one storage medium that is widely available and can be relatively efficient. Hydrogen is the universal medium that "stores" all forms of renewable energy to assure that a stable and reliable supply is available for power generation and, equally important, for transport.

As a carrier of energy—but definitely not a source—hydrogen is neither stable nor reliable. The notion of stability is dismissed with a single word: Hindenburg. The hype about hydrogen is extreme and extremely ridiculous.

Transporting hydrogen is prohibitively expensive and requires distillates of crude oil. In addition, automakers will not make hydrogen fuel-cell cars until the hydrogen infrastructure is in place, and the infrastructure will not appear until there are a sufficient number of fuel-cell cars on the road.

4. *Using Internet technology to transform the power grid of every continent into an energy sharing intergrid that acts just like the Internet. The reconfiguration of the world's power grid, along the lines of the internet, allowing businesses and homeowners to produce their own energy and share it with each other, is just now being tested by power companies in Europe. The new smart grids or intergrids will revolutionize the way electricity is produced and delivered. Millions of existing and new buildings—homes, offices, factories—will be converted or built to serve as "positive power plants" that can capture local renewable energy—solar, wind, geothermal, biomass, hydro, and ocean waves—to create electricity to power the buildings, while sharing the surplus power with others across smart intergrids, just like we now produce our own information and share it with each other across the Internet.*

Never mind the endless hopium associated with producing "renewable" energy for more than seven billion people. Never mind the war-based industrial economy of the world's sole remaining superpower. If we're counting on technology currently under testing in Europe, we're also assuming Europe will exist as a political entity for a long time. We're also assuming Europeans will continue to play nice with each other as well as people in other countries. The very idea of surplus power is being revealed as a horrifically bad joke as the Middle East and northern Africa come under daily attack from several more-industrialized nations.

5. *Transitioning the transport fleet to electric, plug in and fuel cell vehicles that can buy and sell electricity on a smart continental interactive power grid. The electricity we produce in our buildings from renewable energy will also be used to power electric plug-in cars or to create hydrogen to power fuel cell vehicles. The electric plug in vehicles, in turn, will also serve as portable power plants that can sell electricity back to the main grid.*

Car culture is a huge source of many of our worst problems. Cheering for the never-ending continuation of car culture is a death sentence for the living planet. In addition, as indicated above, transporting hydrogen is unsafe, expensive, and dependent upon distillates of crude oil. And then there's that chicken-and-egg issue associated with construction of infrastructure to support hydrogen fuel-cell cars.

When these five pillars come together, they make up an indivisible technological platform—an emergent system whose properties and functions are qualitatively different from the sum of its parts. In other words, the synergies between the pillars create a new economic paradigm that can transform the world.

When these five pillars of sand come together, they make up an undistinguished pile of dysfunctional hopium—a pile of sand whose properties and functions are qualitatively and quantitatively irrelevant to the industrial economy. In other words, the synergies between the meaningless pillars create a new pile of false hope for those who wish to continue destroying the living world. Fortunately, the hopium is running out.

Contrary to conventional wisdom among civilized humans, we don't need an industrial economy to survive. In fact, all evidence indicates the opposite is true, yet we keep cheering for this culture of death, cheering for continued destruction of all we need for our survival. Insanity has won, proving Ralph Waldo Emerson correct: "The end of the human race will be that it will eventually die of civilization."

PLAYING COURT JESTER

Quoting Carl Sagan, I begin some presentations with this line: "It is far better to grasp the universe as it really is than to persist in delusion, however satisfying and reassuring." But in the wake of a recent trip to the northeastern United States, it's clear many people disagree with Sagan, choosing delusion over reality, believing we can have infinite growth on a finite planet with no consequences for humans or other organisms, smoking the crack pipe of hopium.

From those who actually absorb my messages about collapse and climate change, I'm asked: "Why bother? Why do you go on the road?"

My response:

Do I tell the truth, or not? Paradoxically, the importance of my messages and my ability to deliver them in compelling fashion are not the primary reasons I spend time on the road. People want to hear what I've done to prepare, so that's why I'm invited to speak. But the real reason I travel is that I need to get away, in large part because the project has failed. I've conducted many experiments, and I know failure when it whacks me in the head.

My experiences, essays, and presentations have failed to promote resistance sufficient to cause collapse of the industrial economy, and have therefore failed to delay human extinction. Further, I've failed to convince even a very small minority of people in my audiences to change their lives. Worse yet, the mud hut offers no viable future for humans, thus precluding a decent future for the youngster here and his generation. Thus, my primary targets—the general public and the youngster and his generation—are left not in the cold but in the extreme heat.

In summary, I recognize the mud hut has become a near-term death trap because of climate chaos, and so I must leave it. And then, when I become totally burned out on the road, demoralized by the majority people in the audiences and the sheer insanity of speaking to a world that will not listen, I must return to the mud hut. And not so much to recover or re-energize as to take my turn at the chores while preparing for another round of insanity.

On the road, there's little possibility to develop a lasting relationship. I throw a Molotov cocktail into the conversation, and then I leave the area.

On the road, I describe how we live at the mud hut. I describe the importance of living for today. I contemplate the ethics of near-term human extinction. In response, I am given nicknames. The latest, which I greatly appreciate: Guy McStinction.

Of course it's not all bad. I enjoy being hosted by people who open their doors, minds, and hearts to me. I enjoy serious conversation about serious topics, always laced with abundant humor.

Shortly after my return from a speaking tour, a comment comes from the ether (to protect the guilty, I'll not reveal names): "Listened to Guy last night. He spoke at our permaculture meeting. It's hard to keep on believing it matters when it really doesn't. We're screwed, no matter what."

The online response from a former fan of mine: "Really, so Guy traveled to your permaculture meeting and left you with the impression we are all screwed no matter what we do? Doesn't sound very motivating towards being proactive. What is the point of having a massive carbon footprint flying about and having people drive to hear him spreading a message if you spread such pessimism that people do not think it matters what we do?"

And in a subsequent message from the latter person: "You were someone I really looked up to last year. Nothing wrong with facing doom head on and naming it for what it is but at least then you gave some hope and some direction, now, not so much."

I've come to the conclusion that hope is hopeless. As Nietzsche pointed out, "hope in reality is the worst of all evils because it prolongs the torments of man." To put Ed Abbey's spin on it, "action is the antidote to despair." So, even though I no longer think my actions matter for humans, I'll take action.

From my email inbox comes a message from the campus "green" committee that invited my presentation at a local college: "We are as alarmed as you are but strongly disagree with your analysis that the only solution to climate chaos is to embrace economic collapse. There are other empowering, creative, sustainable and hopeful courses of action. Our students need to hear these choices in order to move forward. A message entirely consisting of gloom and doom will not move us in a positive direction. If we are to have a future, we must stay engaged, not disempowered and filled with despair."

A portion of my response:

I understand wanting to promote empowerment, creativity, and hopefulness. I cannot understand promoting these attributes in the absence of—or at the expense of—factual information supported by extensive, rational analyses.

Near-term human extinction is a difficult pill to swallow, as is economic collapse. But ignoring ugly truths does not make them any less true. Despair is an expected and appropriate response to this information. Recognizing, accepting, and moving beyond despair are important subsequent steps.

As I indicated in my presentation, only complete economic collapse prevents runaway greenhouse. We've known this tidbit since 2009, when Timothy Garrett's excellent analysis was published in the journal Climatic Change. *It's not as if I'm making up the dire information, or cheering for the human suffering that is resulting from collapse. But I'm not interested in presenting information based on wishful thinking, either.*

On and on it goes. As George Orwell pointed out, "truth is treason in an empire of lies." A typically absurd comment comes from a leading public figure in response to a question about my reporting of the climate science: "I think his view is profoundly disempowering. Whether or not he's right, I think telling people that is not helpful. It's a recipe for ending up with people doing none of the things that are possible to make a difference. There's so much uncertainty in the models that we can't realistically make predictions like that anyway. Climate is highly non-linear, we don't understand the various feedback loops, or where we lie within them, or the net effect of different ones, or the impact of methane in comparison with carbon dioxide, or the background cycle of natural forcings, or the impact of economic collapse on both emissions and global dimming etc etc. I think we need to plan to get over the first hurdle (financial crisis) and then deal with the next, and the one after that as they arise. Relocalization, undertaken for reasons of finance and energy contraction, will also be the only factor that can genuinely benefit climate as well. Whatever reason we do it for, that is the answer—a simpler society."

Let's move toward a simpler society, and the sooner the better. But let's not deal with predicaments as hurdles to be leaped over or knocked down. Let's take them on now, and let's get to the root of the matter: Industrial civilization is destroying life on Earth. Rather than pondering how we can protect faux wealth as the industrial economy unwinds—the leading question for the civilized among us—let's get to work saving the living planet by terminating industrial civilization.

Apparently I disempower people by encouraging them to take responsibility for facts, and for themselves. Oh, the irony. I induce disempowerment and despair. As individuals, we've never had significant power, our privilege aside. For most of us, the limited power we possess has been used primarily to accrue more personal power at the expense of the living planet and people outside the industrialized world.

What of despair? If you don't despair what we've done, and what we continue to do, to the living planet and people outside the industrialized world, I have little sympathy for you. Despair is a typical and expected reaction to my presentations, and I would have it no other way. If the truth causes despair, then bring on the truth. I've been despairing for years. It hurts. But avoiding our emotions makes us less human, hence degrades our humanity. I want no part of that. I want to feel, even when it hurts. Until I can't.

How difficult it is for civilized humans to comprehend that this civilization, like all others, has disadvantages. How difficult it is for civilized humans to comprehend that this civilization, like all others, must end. How difficult it is for civilized humans to comprehend that humans, like other organisms, are headed for extinction.

And you believe I'm not grieving? You believe I enjoy the knowledge in my head? Apparently you've not been paying attention.

Lest you conclude this essay is a defensive rant—and perhaps it is, at least in part—I'm actually going somewhere. All this speaking and writing and reacting and pondering leads me to a new and different place than I ever imagined. Specifically, I'm adjusting to my new roles as the world burns: court jester and psychotherapist. I have no experience with either pursuit, unless playing class clown contributes to the former. But I think Nero had the right idea, creating art as Rome burned. So I'll create humor while taking advantage of opportunities to comfort the afflicted and afflict the comfortable. Perhaps if I provide enough humor, I'll be spared the usual end-of-life experience proposed for those messengers who bring bad news.

Had the industrial economy collapsed in late 2008 or early 2009, as appeared likely at the time, our species might have persisted a few more generations. Now, however, it's time to let go. As individuals, we do not possess the power to alter the outcome. However, we have the power to control

144 Guy R. McPherson

our reaction to events. Thus, the new role I've assigned myself.

I'll present dire information with empathy while promoting resistance. I'll continue to criticize society while empathizing with individuals. And I'll ask people to empathize, and to feel. Even though it hurts.

Why? Because, hopium aside, Carl Sagan was correct: painful reality trumps satisfying, reassuring delusion.

LET GO, OR BE DRAGGED

Contrary to the response of many people to my messages, I'm not suggesting we quit. Giving up is not giving in: Accepting our fate is not synonymous with jumping into the absurdly omnicidal main stream. Just because we're opossums on the roadway doesn't mean we should play possum. Resistance is fertile, after all. To employ a bit of The Boss: "In the end what you don't surrender, well the world just strips away."

Or, to employ a bit of Zen: Let go, or be dragged.

Or, to employ a bit of popular culture: Carpe diem.

Or, to employ a bit of Nietzsche: "Live as though the day were here." To which I would add, "first, do no harm."

Climate chaos is well under way, and has become irreversible over temporal spans relevant to humans because of positive feedbacks. Such is the nature of reaching the acceleration phase of the nonlinear system that is climate catastrophe.

As a result of ongoing, accelerating climate change, I'm letting go of the notion that *Homo sapiens* will inhabit this planet beyond 2030 or so. I'm letting go of the notion that *Homo sapiens* will inhabit this verdant little valley at the edge of American Empire after it turns to dust within a very few years. I'm letting go of the notion that, within a few short years, there will remain any habitat for humans in the interior of any large continent in the northern hemisphere.

I'm letting go of the notion we'll retain even a fraction of one percent of the species currently on Earth beyond 2050. But I'm not letting go of the notion of resistance, which is a moral imperative.

I no longer judge people for buying into cultural conditioning. For example, it's far easier to live in a city, at the height of civilization's excesses, than not. I know how easy it is to live in a city surrounded by beautiful distractions and pleasant interactions, and I fully understand the costs and consequences of dwelling there, as well as the price to be paid in the near future. I spent about half my life in various cities, and I understand the physical ease and existential pain of living at the apex of empire. Also, I know all about the small joys and great pains associated with living in the country. I spent the other half of my life in the country and in towns with fewer than 1,000 people. I understand why the country bumpkin is assigned stereotypical labels related to ignorance and, paradoxically, self-reliance.

It's clearly too late to tear down this irredeemably corrupt system and realize any substantive benefits for humans or other organisms. And yet I strongly agree with activist Lierre Keith: "The task of an activist is not to navigate systems of oppressive power with as much personal integrity as possible; it is to dismantle those systems." If it seems I'm filled with contradictions, color me hypocritical (i.e., fully human) in a Walt Whitman sort of way: "Do I contradict myself? Very well, then I contradict myself, I am large, I contain multitudes."

Our remaining time on this orb is too short to cast aspersions at those who live differently from ourselves, as most people in industrialized countries have done throughout their lives. Most people in the industrialized world became cultural crack babies in the womb. There is little hope to break the addiction of ingestion at this late point in the era of industry, and I'm throwing in the towel on changing the minds of typically mindless Americans. No longer will I try to convince people to give up the crack pipe based on my perception of morality reality.

I'll continue to speak. I'll continue to write. But these efforts will be presented with less urgency than I've previously employed, and they will represent personal perspectives and actions. I'll no longer recommend to others the path I've taken.

Nietzsche's comment about seizing the day, every day, brings to mind the final words of Joseph Campbell's 1949 book, *The Hero with a Thousand Faces*:

It is not society that is to guide and save the creative hero, but precisely the reverse. And so every one of us shares the supreme ordeal—carries the cross of the redeemer—not in the bright moments of his tribe's great victories, but in the silences of his personal despair.

With the preceding dire news in mind, it would be easy to forget how fortunate we are. After all, we get to die. That simple fact alone is cause for celebration because it indicates we get to live. As I've written many times, our knowledge of DNA assures us that the odds any one of us existing are greater than the odds against being a particular grain of sand on all the world's beaches. No, the odds are much greater than that: they exceed the odds of being a single atom plucked from the entire universe. To quote the evolutionary biologist Richard Dawkins, "In the teeth of these stupefying odds it is you and I that are privileged to be here, privileged with eyes to see where we are and brains to wonder why."

No surrender

Occupy. Idle No More. Anarchism. Relocalization. Going "back to the land. "

What do they share in common? They are beyond the mainstream. As a result, I'm a fan. Only dead fish swim with the main stream.

Following contemporary culture gets us Orwellian endless wars that benefit the financially wealthy while impoverishing and killing the rest of us. Following contemporary culture leads directly to the Sixth Great Extinction. Following contemporary culture tips us further into human-population overshoot on an overcrowded planet. Following contemporary culture brings us a system that fouls the air and dirties the water. Following contemporary culture leads to the inability to distinguish needs from wants. Following contemporary culture ratchets up climate chaos to the point of near-term human extinction.

Most people I know don't merely follow contemporary culture. They promote it. They promote death. They promote destruction. Holding onto the wishful thinking that permeates the misguided American Dream, they promote whatever it takes to get "ahead." Ahead of the neighbors, local and global, for a few dollars more. A few dollars more, to pay for a night out. And to buy more toys, of course. Always more toys.

James Truslow Adams popularized the notion of the American Dream in his 1931 book, *The Epic of America*. The Dream he popularized bears little resemblance to the keeping-up-with-the-Joneses approach exhibited by the vast majority of contemporary Americans. After all, the dream popularized and promoted by Adams was one in which Americans would "devote themselves to the 'Great Society'...We cannot become a great democracy by giving ourselves up as individuals to selfishness, physical comfort, and cheap amusements. The very foundation of the American dream of a better and richer life for all is that all, in varying degrees, shall be capable of wanting to share in it. It can never be wrought into reality by cheap people or by 'keeping up with the Joneses.'"

The society I've known my entire life has been dominated by cheap people who spend their lives seeking physical comfort and cheap amusements. My path from baby boomer to adult doomer results in large part from my recognition that industrial civilization is a culture of death. We treat as our birthright personal automobiles, clean water coming out the taps, inexpensive food at the grocery stores, and grid-tied electricity. That the most lethal killing force in the history of the world is needed to maintain these "rights" rarely enters the mind. That the costs of physical comforts and cheap amusements for the few include stealing from other species, other cultures, and future generations of industrial humans rarely enters the mind. If that's not horrific enough, consider the consequences of our here-today, screw-tomorrow attitude with respect to using radioactive materials to power our televisions.

If you're seeking a single example of how the mainstream promotes living for today at the expense of future life on this planet, you could do worse than nuclear power plants. The half-life of Uranium-238 is 4.5 billion years, which is approximately the age of Earth. We have yet to develop the means of storing or discarding the resulting waste.

I can imagine no worse strategy than the one we're struggling to maintain. Even as industrial civilization teeters on the brink, we applaud all efforts to keep it from tipping over the edge. We applaud the loss of the U.S. Constitution and Bill of Rights. We applaud oppression abroad, including the efficiency of drone-bombing people of color. The occasional U.S. citizen caught in the cross-hairs is tolerated as collateral damage. We applaud whole-sale destruction of the living planet on which we depend for our survival.

This way of living is the only way we've ever known. Driven by fear of the unknown, most of us accept omnicide as our default strategy. I propose another route.

Actually, I propose any other route. I practice an economy of gifts within agrarian anarchy. I live close to the land and close to my neighbors, human and otherwise. But I promote Occupy, Idle No More, relocalization, and *any* other way of living beyond the mainstream. In short, I promote all of the above, largely because the current set of living arrangements is utter disaster. It would be difficult to conjure up a worse way to live, even if we tried.

WHAT ARE WE FIGHTING FOR?

I've often mentioned, verbally and in writing, two phenomena I've long believe are worth fighting for: the living planet and freedom based in anarchy. I surrender. I no longer believe the struggle matters on either front.

I no longer think we'll save the remaining shards of the living planet beyond another human generation. We'll destroy every—or nearly every—species on Earth when the positive feedbacks associated with climate change come more seriously into play.

The climate-change data, models, and assessments keep coming at us, like waves crashing on a rocky, indifferent beach. The worst drought in 800 years in the western United States is met by levels of societal ignorance and political silence I've come to expect. I would be stunned if this valley—or any other area in the interior of a northern-hemisphere continent—will provide habitat for humans five years from now. And climate change is only part of the story.

My trademark optimism vanishes when I realize that, in addition to climate chaos, we're on the verge of tacking on ionizing radiation from the world's nuclear power plants, which number more than 400. Let's ignore for now the radioactive waste we've left lying around without a plan or already dumped into the world's oceans. When we choke on our own poison, we'll be taking the whole ship down with us, spewing a global blanket of radiation in the wake of collapse. Can we kill every single species on Earth? Apparently we're willing to give it a try, and I will not be surprised by our "success" at this omnicidal endeavor.

Onto anarchy. Few people understand what it is, and even fewer support it. As a product of cultural conditioning, the typical American confuses anarchy with terrorism. Considering the near-term exit of *Homo sapiens* from this planet, it seems a bit ridiculous of me to express concern about living outside the absurdity that has become mainstream.

Color me non-judgmental. Continue to fuck the planet and our future, and see if I give a damn. Actually, saying we fucked the future without offering so much as a kiss is an insult to four-letter words everywhere. Minor efforts to sound the alarm, including my own, fade to insignificance when compared to the juggernaut of global imperialism. These efforts have long been irrelevant; it's my awakening that is new.

And color me sad, of course, at the societal path we've taken. Swept up in the pursuit of *more* instead of *better*, we've become the waves approaching the rocky shore.

We had an opportunity to return to our tribal roots, as others have done when civilizations collapsed. Consider, for example, the survivors from the Olmec, Chaco, and Mimbres cultures, all of whom chose tribalism when civilization failed. They demonstrated that civilization is a cul-de-sac, but not a one-way street. Tribalism worked for two million years in a diverse array of situations. It worked before and after civilizations arose in specific regions. For many decades, our version of civilization has been successful only for a few individuals of one species, yet we keep tinkering with the system long after it's failed.

Despite considerable evidence to the contrary, we've come to believe industrial civilization is the only way to live. As we'll soon discover, it's the only way to die, at least at the level of our species.

Inspired by Kurt Vonnegut's eponymous poem, I offer the following requiem for Earth.

If Earth could sing with a female voice.

Her strength would be evident, though her tone might waver.

Could she withhold judgment against one of her own,

through all we've done to her, and our brethren?

We lived in her bosom from which we were born

for two million years not forsaking our home.

Then we became something different from all we had known,

and in the gasp of a breath we destroyed it all.

Can you blame her for judging us, considering what we've done?

She gave us every chance to turn it around.

Now we're all done and she's endured our abuse,

including pillage, plunder, and rape without any excuse.

All she can sing in that mournful tone is sorrow for the
    power she unleashed,

through us and thus dispassionately onto herself, destroyed
    by one of her own.

She must ponder how our hubris overwhelmed our humility

in concluding about our recent selves: They didn't like it here.

ONLY LOVE REMAINS

Most people would say I'm not religious. I'm not spiritually religious, although I exhibit some behaviors in a religious manner. I refer to myself as a free-thinker, a skeptic, and occasionally an indifferent agnostic or a militant atheist. So the apparently spiritual title of this essay would seem out of character for those who know me.

I'll not wander down the road of knowing me. Even after five decades of study, much of it characterized by the serious introspection allowed those who pursue the life of the mind in the halls of academia, I barely know myself. And I know too little about love. But I'm pretty certain it's all we have.

I've tried turning my back on my own emotions, and those of others. I've been a rationalist most of my life, and my entire career was spent as a scientist and teacher. My laser-like focus on reason precluded the ready expression of feelings, an attitude reinforced by the culture in which I came of age, a culture in which the only thing worse than having feelings was expressing them. For most of my life I've been mystified by public displays of affection and people who mourned the loss of individual lives.

After all, as I've known for a long time, birth is lethal. Nobody gets out alive, a notion that applies to cultures and species as well as individuals. My perceived lack of empathy led some to conclude I was a sociopath. Or a psychopath.

My two-sizes-too-small brain can't customarily distinguish the two.

Long familiar with his talent as a guitarist, I didn't think the words of Jimi Hendrix applied to my world: "When the power of love overcomes the love of power the world will know peace." Recently I've begun to question my earlier sentiments.

Heartbroken, again and again

I keep believing I've worked through each of the five Kubler-Ross stages of grief. And then, just when my rational side seems to get the upper hand, I'm overwhelmed again and thrust back to the lobby of my own personal Heartbreak Hotel.

A decade ago, as I was editing a book on climate change, I realized we had triggered events likely to cause human extinction by 2030 or so. Notwithstanding neoconservative talking points (aka lies) to the contrary, burning fossil fuels that accumulated over millions of years within the span of a couple centuries is having expectedly horrific impacts on the environment we share with millions of other species. Recognizing the horrors we've triggered, I mourned for months, to the bewilderment of the three people who noticed. Shortly thereafter, I was elated to learn about a hail-Mary pass that just might allow our persistence for a few more generations: Peak oil and its economic consequences might bring the industrial economy to an overdue close, just in time to allow our species to persist beyond another generation.

It's been a rollercoaster ride since then. Oil priced at $147.27 back in 2008 nearly sent the world's industrial economy into the abattoir. Close, but no life-ring. Even as increasingly dire data, models, and climate-change assessments roll in, politicians and central bankers have kept the wheels of industry churning. Although we've been in the midst of an economic depression for several years, atmospheric carbon dioxide levels keep rising to record-setting levels each year.

Finally, I surrender. We're done. *Homo colossus* has tripped more than a dozen positive-feedback triggers, any one of which leads to near-term human extinction. The combination is truly lethal.

Now what?

I abandoned the luxury-filled, high-pay, low-work position I loved as a tenured full professor to go back to the land. I led by example. Vanishingly few followed. I'm reminded of the prescient words attributed to American existential psychologist Rollo May: "The opposite of courage in our society is not cowardice, it is conformity."

My new path presented tremendous challenges for a life-long academic who could barely distinguish between a screwdriver and a zucchini. I learned new skills, including rough carpentry, plumbing, masonry, gardening, and animal husbandry. Learning by doing, my naivety produced injuries to my body and my psyche. Even before I broke my ribs and suffered numerous minor scrapes and bruises, most of my colleagues concluded I'd gone insane. This conclusion was shared by many of my friends and family members.

I no longer communicate with most of those colleagues, friends, and family. It's too difficult to justify the occasional conversation.

As an academic conservation biologist, I've long recognized that the living planet sustains our species. I was pointing out the dark underbelly of industrial civilization even as we were driving some 200 species to extinction every day. But I was ensconced in the underbelly, too. Living at the apex of empire, a large city in the southwestern United States, meant compartmentalizing my life. Even as I was teaching the horrors of how we live, I kept living in that horrifying manner. Through years of intrapersonal conflict, love rarely crossed my mind.

The tide rises

I miss teaching, of course. I miss the honors students and inmates with whom I regularly worked. We sought meaningful lives of excellence, and I committed my life to service, primarily to people too-often underserved by an irredeemably corrupt system. Along the way, I learned empathy and love from my students. I suspect some of them learned, too.

But I could not continue to enjoy the city life and face the mirror each day. Such are the hazards of knowledge. Ignorance is bliss but, contrary to the daily choices of the typical American consumer, bliss is overrated.

Eventually, I began to remove the cultural shackles that bound me. Living and working in a sparsely populated rural area these last four years has provided ample time to think, and think deeply, as I have developed new skills and a new perspective. Surrounded by Earth's bounty and beauty, transformation befell me. More than four years after I moved out of Tucson, Arizona, only a few hours in any city induces depression.

Now my wife and I share a small property at the edge of empire with another couple and their young son. We raise chickens and ducks for eggs, and goats provide our milk and cheese. A large orchard complements several large gardens near the off-grid, straw-bale duplex we inhabit. We are committed to working with other members of our human community as we muddle through a future characterized by collapse on all fronts, economic, environmental, and climatic included.

This is not an easy existence, especially relative to my life in the hallowed halls of academia. But it has its own rewards, foremost among them immersion into the real, natural world and an appreciative, loving human community.

The high tide of love

Finally, more than a half-century into a largely unexamined life, I have come to love humanity and the living planet. The wisdom of Jimi Hendrix, long hidden beneath the cultural programming one would expect in the backwoods, redneck logging town of my youth, nags at me.

The living planet and a decent human community sustain each of us, whether we realize it or not. Our years on this most wondrous of planets, regardless how numerous they are, are to be celebrated.

After all, we get to die, and that makes us the lucky ones. It means we get to live. As I indicated in a previous essay, our knowledge of DNA informs us that the odds against any one of us being here exceed the odds of being a single atom plucked from the entire universe.

The privilege to be here, on this life-giving planet at this astonishing time in human history, is sufficient to inspire awe in the most uncaring of individuals. At this late juncture in the age of industry, at the dawn of our day on Earth, we still have love: love for each other, love for our children and grandchildren, love for nature. One could argue it is all we have left.

Those who pull the levers in this life-destroying culture care about power to a far greater extent than they care about love. This culture will not know peace. It is much too late for love to extend our run as a culture or a species—too late to employ the wisdom of Jimi Hendrix—but love surely offers redemption to individual humans.

Will we, as individuals, know peace? That's up to us. I suggest most of us will know peace only when we find ourselves lying helpless in the broken arms of our doomed Earth.

Would you like to see your manuscript become a book?

If you are interested in becoming a PublishAmerica author, please submit your manuscript for possible publication to us at:

mybook@publishamerica.com

You may also mail in your manuscript to:

**PublishAmerica
PO Box 151
Frederick, MD 21705**

www.publishamerica.com

CPSIA information can be obtained at www.ICGtesting.com
Printed in the USA
LVOW10s1258120914

403784LV00001B/20/P